REORGANIZATION AND RENEWAL:

STRATEGIES FOR HEALTHCARE LEADERS

REORGANIZATION AND RENEWAL:

STRATEGIES FOR HEALTHCARE LEADERS

Donald N. Lombardi

Health Administration Press
Chicago, Illinois

01 00 99 98 97   5 4 3 2 1

Library of Congress Cataloging-in-Publication Data

Lombardi, Donald N., 1956–
    Reorganization and Renewal: Strategies for Healthcare Lead-
ers / by Donald N. Lombardi.
        p. cm.
    Includes bibliographical references and index.
    ISBN 1-56793-062-X
    1. Health facilities—Administration.   2. Corporate reorganizations.
I. Title.
    [DNLM: 1. Health Facilities—organization & administration.   2. Orga-
nizational Innovation.   3. Hospital Restructuring.   WX 150 L842f 1997]
RA971.L65 1997
362.1'068—dc21
DNLM/DLC
for Library of Congress   97-18702
                                                                     CIP

The paper used in this publication meets the minimum requirements of American
National Standards for Information Sciences—Permanence of Paper for Printed
Library Materials, ANSI Z39.48–1984. ∞ ™

Health Administration Press
A division of the Foundation of the
    American College of Healthcare Executives
One North Franklin Street
Chicago, IL 60606–3491
312/424–2800

To Deborah Ann

CONTENTS

FOREWORD

In adapting to the new requirements of managed care, the healthcare industry continues its dramatic pace of change. The search is now on for the best ways to provide optimum healthcare in the face of potential Medicare and Medicaid reductions and continued fiscal pressure from HMOs. The tools and techniques of reengineering and restructuring have helped achieve record levels of performance for many facilities and have also increased their competitiveness and realized dramatic cost savings; although many organizations have undertaken such campaigns, some have found that they have changed as much as they can, while some even believe they have compromised the quality of their care

Public policy has begun to shift and is now addressing some of the problems that managed care has created. HMOs are finding themselves in the eye of a publicity storm, and although some might initially think this diverts attention from hospitals and integrated healthcare delivery systems, nothing could be farther from the truth. Our two-decade-long emphasis on cost and efficiency has threatened the public's trust in healthcare organizations. This lack of trust could not have come at a worse time: The past several years have seen increasing numbers of organizations forced to dismiss staff and redesign entire divisions. Employees and patients alike cannot help but wonder if their local hospital is capable not only of offering excellent healthcare services but caring about the needs of the community.

Furthermore, the past few years have seen an increase in new organizations and networks cobbled together from formerly independent hospitals, home health agencies, and nursing homes. These emerging networks are searching for ways to use their new organizational power to preserve their core values while trying to realize their full potential. Much expectation has been raised in communities as efforts to promote mergers and affiliations have been pursued. These organizations are faced with the need for future strategies that build on the successes of the past but recognize the continued pressure on resources and quality.

Where do we go from here? Is there one best way to balance economic and business realities with the trust given a healthcare facility by its employees and its patients? The strategies outlined by Don Lombardi in *Reorganization and Renewal: Strategies for Healthcare Leaders* provide a practical framework for healthcare executives to begin and oversee their organizations' restructuring process. Rooted in the principles of planning, the development of timelines and schedules, and enhanced communication skills, this book outlines many proven techniques to preserve trust and improve employee morale. Bolstered by the author's experience consulting more than one hundred healthcare facilities undergoing change, this book is far from being a theoretical discussion of how to manage reengineering and reconstruction. *Reorganization and Renewal* offers a series of practical, proven assessment techniques, from an innovative employee opinion survey to a job analysis worksheet to a list of "do's and don'ts" for the healthcare manager. These instruments will provide valuable data to healthcare organizations as they assess the present and look to the future. Recognizing that the traditional modes of communication are not enough in these times of change, the author offers new methods on how to interact with staff as well as the outlying community.

You will read a case study of a fictional organization—though based on the experiences of real-life facilities—that was forced to reorganize and renew itself. There are also several examples taken from other institutions all on different points of the renewal path, and you will learn of their struggle and their successes. All of this will provide a road map to you as a healthcare executive.

This book recognizes that relationships among healthcare professionals are the key to the future. You will learn how to identify and motivate your "superstar" employees—the backbone of the organization—and use them to help the institutional renewal. You will learn how to increase productivity by identifying the "nonplayers" in your organization and the best ways to make those individuals contribute or move them out of the organization quickly and efficiently. There is even an appendix, "Managing Nonplayer Resistance to Change," that lists twenty lines that "nonplayers" offer during times of change to derail the reconstruction process, along with twenty strategies to defuse and overcome that resistance.

In addition, this book describes and analyzes the benefits of five different organizational models an institution can choose to restructure itself as: the product-line, action-line, decentralized-decision, triad, and traditional models.

Everybody working in healthcare institutions today should read this book. It will both inspire and provide useful ideas that you can use to manage change and lead effectively during the next decade of healthcare delivery. For some readers, this book will feel like a return to basics: Many of its ideas are rooted in the reality that, in the end, an organization's performance results from the cumulative performance of its staff. Ultimately, improving every employee's performance is the best strategy for improving an organization's performance. This book is not a criticism of reengineering or restructuring but rather a recognition that we are on a journey, and the next phase of that journey is renewal. It is an exciting phase—and an essential one—and I encourage you to read this book and begin the next phase of your journey of change as you deliver the best possible healthcare to your communities.

Joseph P. Ross,
President, Shore Health System, Inc.

ACKNOWLEDGMENTS

As this is my eighth book, I would feel remiss if I did not thank my parents for instilling a respect for learning and love of reading in me from my first memories to now. Additionally, my two uncles, Colonel H. C. Roberson, USMC, and Fr. Nicholas D. Lombardi, S.J., made certain that I read and thought about what I read. I am proud and happy to say that all four are still "on the job" today, in this and every regard.

A special note of thanks to Craig Roberson for another great initial editing job, and as always, my wife Deborah Ann ran the show as the book took shape. Health Administration Press helped to conceptualize and produce this book.

I am quite fortunate to have the contributions of all of my family and friends in healthcare.

THE HEALTHCARE RENEWAL IMPERATIVE

At every level throughout the healthcare industry, the words "restructuring" and "downsizing" have become part of the vocabulary of healthcare executives and managers. Although downsizing has unfortunately become a part of everyday life for millions of Americans, this phenomenon did not until recently extend to the healthcare industry. Healthcare institutions were insulated from downsizing by financial reimbursement from the government, ardent community support, and a lack of competition, all important factors in keeping healthcare institutions immune. This, however, is no longer true.

Healthcare institutions are looking more closely at restructuring to keep their organizations solvent. Although restructuring entails employee layoffs and a reduction in services, which can ultimately affect the basic health of a consumer community, it can allow a healthcare organization to address more effectively and pragmatically the needs of that community. A healthcare organization that is structured more progressively as a business entity, while embracing new technology and a larger spectrum of services, is one that will not only survive in the future but actually thrive as customer/patient needs grow and intensify.

The Spotlight Era of healthcare is now upon us, and healthcare organizations will be more closely scrutinized than ever before (see Figure 1.1). The popular media has embraced healthcare as a savory topic for discussion in nightly television broadcasts and daily newspaper articles, and this coverage is rarely positive. For example, the front page of *USA Today* recently featured a graph indicating that over 30 percent

Figure 1.1 The Spotlight Era of Healthcare

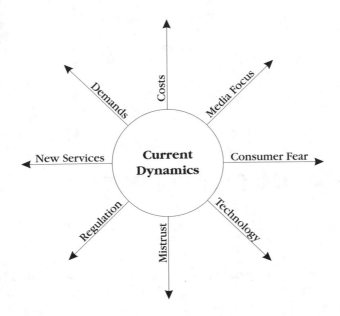

of individuals facing surgery fear poor treatment by healthcare workers. Further, the respondents' major fear—indicated by over 54 percent—was that surgery would not correct the problem. Both of these indicators help to create the perception that healthcare institutions are both less than charitable when working with patients and do not provide services as effectively as they should.

Another example of negative media coverage can be seen in a popular type of article run by virtually every major newspaper across the country. In the prototypical article, hospital CEOs' salaries are exhibited to show that their compensation level is still relatively high despite the fact that hospitals are downsizing and medical costs are rapidly rising.

The Spotlight Era is also predicated on the miracles that are being promised by healthcare institutions. Technological advances have occurred in healthcare more rapidly than in almost any other industry, and this has led to an escalation of customer/patient expectations. Individuals now expect a healthcare organization to provide a wide assortment of services instantaneously at an extremely low cost. This combination of increased expectations with new technology can lead to a natural need for rightsizing as consumers want more value and the latest technology, which can often replace human workers. It also suggests a need for a renewal of the healthcare organizational model.

Healthcare organizations must be more competitive now than ever before. Mergers and acquisitions have become the order of the day, and hospitals that previously competed against one another are now partners in the change process. Clinics and alternative healthcare organizations are now either merging or becoming part of the larger umbrella provided by a major medical center or large community hospital. As this occurs, healthcare executives look to cut their human resources budget to realize necessary savings and to eliminate duplication of services and personnel. This increase in competition has also evidenced itself not only in local mergers and acquisitions but in the emergence of several national healthcare entities. These national chains own and operate facilities across the country under the aegis of one predominant corporate entity that sets standards and policies for all of its members. Advertising, marketing, and other business efforts, which were not previously needed, have now become part of daily business practices for virtually all healthcare facilities.

The Spotlight Era of healthcare is also marked by a set of demands placed on the healthcare institution stating that they should not be immune from the societal pressures all businesses face. As other service organizations find themselves in a position to restructure, healthcare institutions, which in the eyes of the public have made money and stayed consistently profitable for years, must look at their bottom-line accountabilities to ensure that they are running "lean and mean" in order to maintain credibility with their local community. As healthcare expenses rise and individuals pay more money for their healthcare coverage through HMOs and other insurance means, consumers naturally become more interested in the way that their local healthcare organization manages costs.

Finally, state and local governments also play a role in healthcare's Spotlight Era. The raging debate over Medicaid and Medicare has affected all healthcare institutions, as the reduction or elimination of these reimbursable services is being considered. State support for indigent care has also dwindled, and as the taxpayers become more wary of how their tax dollars are being spent, healthcare will naturally be called into question. Most individuals believe—incorrectly—that their taxes directly support their local healthcare institution. Because of this misconception, the local organization is erroneously assumed to cause higher taxes, to decrease the quality of governmental services, and to erode the community's trust.

Although these pressures have been present for at least a couple of years in the healthcare industry, there exists an additional set of outside factors that make healthcare organizational renewal necessary.

Examining Extrinsic Forces

Every healthcare manager and leader must understand how extrinsic forces require a healthcare organization to renew itself. These factors include:

- fiscal austerity;
- community perception;
- elimination of services; and
- outmoding of services.

The first and most visible factor is the need for fiscal austerity—the need to save money—as most healthcare professionals recognize that reimbursement is no longer automatic and that individual consumers are paying more for services than ever before. The emergence of HMOs and other alternative payor methods has also affected the fiscal plan of every healthcare organization, while third party payors are prominent in the financial scheme at every business level.

Liability costs have increased exponentially, not only in terms of risk management but in the delivery of basic care, medical malpractice, and an entire host of other legal initiatives that affect liability. The modern healthcare organization must adhere to standards that negate potential liability, and it must be vigilant that its everyday practices comply with an ever-widening range of laws and regulations.

Additionally, new technology costs money. As healthcare organizations strive to keep pace with their competition additional financial investment must be made into the purchase of new equipment and the latest technology.

Another need for fiscal austerity can be found in any community's basic economic scheme: If the major local employer leaves town, for example, the local hospital must spend its resources differently, often more judiciously. If the entire nation is suffering from an economic malaise, the need for fiscal austerity becomes apparent, as the average healthcare institution is perceived as a community public trust and must therefore "sacrifice" along with its business counterparts in the community.

An important point must be made about fiscal austerity. Although it is a very visible factor facing a healthcare organization, it is neither the most important nor most prominent factor mandating a need for organizational renewal. Cutting costs, however, is often presented by executive management to employees as being the main reason for rightsizing or downsizing. While the need to save money is an important symptom, it is not the illness. In fact, using fiscal austerity as the excuse for downsizing can often lead to mistrust and a profound lack of support and commitment to the reorganization process. Therefore, it is extremely important for healthcare leaders to understand all the principal external factors affecting their healthcare organizations.

Community perception, the awareness on the part of the customer/patient that he or she is paying more for services, is the second external factor. This perhaps has more credibility in the minds of healthcare employees, if discussed properly and used as the rationale for creating a new organizational model. An individual working at a manufacturing plant that has been affected by downsizing over recent years can naturally become almost spiteful of a healthcare organization that does not downsize, or at least increase its efforts to meet that manufacturing employee's healthcare needs. This individual has become more aware of a rise in healthcare costs—as seen by greater deductions in monthly paychecks, perhaps, or because of other indicators—and is thus more inquisitive about how the local healthcare institution employs its assets.

Most healthcare consumers do indeed have a certain amount of trust in their healthcare institution, based on personal experience and word-of-mouth advertising. This feeling of trust is jeopardized by healthcare organizations that do not make efficient use of resources and do not attempt to meet the needs of the customer/patient on a daily basis. In analyzing a current community perception, perhaps using the indicators displayed in Figure 1.2, the healthcare leader can garner essential data to help build the model for the renewed healthcare organization.

Figure 1.2   Prevailing Community Sentiment

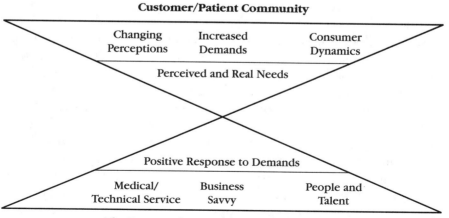

Customer/Patient Community

Changing Perceptions | Increased Demands | Consumer Dynamics

Perceived and Real Needs

Positive Response to Demands

Medical/Technical Service | Business Savvy | People and Talent

The Progressive Healthcare Organization

Mandated elimination of services also takes part in the need for a renewed healthcare organization. The federal government, for example, will not reimburse care in the future as generously as it has in the past, which has become both a political and civic reality for every healthcare organization. Likewise, state governments have begun to regulate uncompensated care practices and other reimbursement methods in a manner not particularly favorable to the healthcare institution. Locally, city and county governments have closed clinics and other auxiliary healthcare delivery facilities—or have merely waited for profit-driven healthcare organizations to absorb or purchase them—as such facilities can represent a major legal risk and often a financial drain on the local civic budget. HMOs have often eliminated services and, in some cases, insurance companies have restricted their coverage for certain procedures. As a result, it is not profitable for the healthcare organization to offer these services, and thus the employees providing them must be laid off or transferred to other divisions where the services are provided or their skills can be used.

Along with the mandated elimination of services, a natural outmoding of functions has occurred. Chemotherapy, for example, is not the arduous and costly process it once was. In some cases, it can be provided on an outpatient basis within a physician's office, rather than an inpatient service at a local hospital. The delivery of subacute care has undergone similar changes. As a result of becoming outmoded, many procedures are no longer cost-effective and can be discontinued, which has led to an increase in reengineering efforts. Healthcare organizations reengineering themselves are trying to answer the question, "If we were to open our business anew today, what would we do differently?"

But for a healthcare organization, this is a specious question. For example, should a hospital located in a resort city—where it is a very visible, well-known entity—close its gambling addiction services, if it maintains a small percentage of clients? Some healthcare organizations would, particularly if a major cost savings could be realized. However, that organization would run the risk of deleterious news coverage, community "fallout," or similar manifestations of negative ill-will. Reengineering outmoded services must be done gingerly, perceptively, and with regard more toward prevailing community sentiment and need than purely financial factors. If healthcare employees become convinced that their organization is strictly "out to make a buck" without regard for community services, an incredible backlash can be created within the organization, which can become particularly combustible when it attempts to renew itself or adopt a new organizational model.

The Intrinsic Change Mandate

Within a healthcare organization, a massive amount of change mandating new organizational models is taking place. Renewal of the organization must address several intrinsic factors, including:

- shift of services;
- specialized and generalized services;
- duplicate responsibilities; and
- executive management.

These are often related to external factors but are more easily recognized by the healthcare employee at every level. In this section, we will explore these intrinsic factors, attempting not only to define them but to prepare communication strategies and other plans that are essential for renewing a healthcare organization.

Inpatient versus Outpatient Services

Predominant among these factors is the shift of inpatient services to outpatient service, which has affected virtually every American healthcare organization over the past ten years. This shift has had several obvious results. Patients spend less time at the hospital, which is of course time efficient as well as cost effective. Traditionally, because average healthcare consumers assess the gravity of their illness on how long they "have to spend in the hospital," an outpatient procedure can alleviate fear, increase credibility with the consumer/patient, and intensify the positive perception of the facility.

However, this shift to outpatient services has several fundamental implications for the healthcare organization. Logically, if people spend less time "in the hospital," the need for support services lessens. Support services such as security, housekeeping, dietitians, and other areas are needed to a lesser degree, and this can lead to layoffs, which if not prevented properly can add to the confusion and fear existent among employees. Furthermore, the shift to outpatient services can result in the closing of entire wards within a hospital, for example, or the entire eradication of a department. Again, without proper communication, based not only on what is happening but *why* it is happening, organizational morale can be devastated by this shift from inpatient to outpatient services—a shift that is not only quite natural but increasingly necessary in the modern healthcare environment. A move to outpatient services is of course predicated on the technological advances that have taken place within the healthcare profession. This advancement of technology has affected healthcare organizations in an assortment of ways:

- computerization, which has extended itself to every conceivable area of a hospital;
- communication, to include the use of telemarketing, telemedicine, e-mail, and other communication devices;
- new medicine, to include everything from new allergy remedies to cutting-edge pharmaceuticals;
- new medicine administration, to include the way that medicine is delivered and ingested by a patient;
- home care, which has become perhaps the ultimate outpatient service;
- alternative medicine, to include chiropractic, holistic healing, spiritually based healing, and other practices new to mainstream American medicine;
- equipment versatility and portability, which now allows seasoned professionals to use equipment outside of the hospital setting;
- new treatments, such as sleep disorder therapy, gambling addiction counseling, and other areas of healing that not only embrace new technology but represent new product lines for the astute healthcare organization; and
- new procedures that include cutting-edge transplanting of organs, heart disease remedies, and other new procedures that are celebrated in the media and then become part of the expectation for the customer/patient.

All of these technological advances promise—or threaten—radical change for traditional healthcare, and they must be considered during the reorganization process.

Specialization and Generalization

Specialization and generalization also affect healthcare organizational renewal. Many hospitals now specialize their services instead of offering traditional, generalized services. Conversely, some hospitals, which previously had been "specialty hospitals," are seeing more patients who need more generalized services. In both cases, it is important for the organization to recognize that the American healthcare consumer wants *all* medical services in a quick, efficient manner. As healthcare organizations renew, the community hospital is in a unique position to capitalize on this need.

Fundamentally, healthcare leaders at every level should make certain that all of their staff members understand that there are three expressions that cannot be used at any time through the reorganization process:

1. **We do not do that here.** The healthcare employee's correct response should be, "We do not offer those services at this particular facility, but we have a partner in the process who does offer these services, and I will orchestrate the action needed for you to receive those services."

2. **That's not my job.** This time-honored excuse must be replaced with, "I will immediately get on the phone with the person who is in charge of that and arrange the services at once."

3. **I don't know.** This alibi must be replaced with, "I will have an answer for you by 3:00 p.m. on that particular question." This answer should be given with the full knowledge that an answer can be garnered by 1:00 p.m. That is, the employee should not overpromise, and thus set expectations unnecessarily for the customer/patient. Rather, the employee must show accountability and demonstrate, through this particular answer, that the patient's needs will be met.

Healthcare consumers are not particularly interested in an organization's agenda of specialization or generalization. What they care about is getting the services that they need immediately. Accordingly, these three responses must be replaced with the alternative response indicated, as both a preparation measure in establishing the renewed organization, as well as in ensuring customer/patient credibility immediately.

Duplicated Responsibilities

As organizations merge, or acquisitions are enacted, a duplication of individual or departmental responsibilities can occur within a healthcare institution. As a result, a certain position can be downsized, or an entire department can be eliminated. This is an unfortunate "necessary evil" in the change process, but one that must be taken into account in the reorganization process nonetheless.

Fundamentally, when a duplication of services or staff is recognized within an organization, five defining elements must be taken into account in deciding which entity will remain:

1. past performance of the two entities, determining which one has demonstrated the best performance, the most efficient service, and the greatest commitment to the organization and its customer/patients;

2. future potential, including willingness to grow and commit to an organization during times of change;

3. the existing customer base, to include current customer relations, market percentages, and other imperative factors relative to established business;

4. future market potential, including the location of the particular entity, its ability to absorb new technology, and its established growth pattern, which can predict future growth and development; and

5. commitment to the renewal mission of the organization, and an emphasis on future action as opposed to past performance.

The worst mistake that can be made in the reorganization process is to retain individuals who have long tenure but questionable performance. By using appropriate performance evaluation measures—and by using these five questions to decide which entities and individuals will be part of the renewed organization—an organization can increase credibility with its customer/patients as well as reinforce the integrity between the employees and organizational leadership.

Executive Management

Finally, a shift in executive management or mission can lead to strong internal change within an organization. A new CEO, for example, has a natural opportunity to renew his or her organization, as we will see throughout this book. It is additionally important, however, for the CEO not only to present a new vision, but additionally a new mission, credo, and employee handbook, and to increase efforts in four areas relative to executive leadership:

1. communication;
2. leadership;
3. decision making; and
4. knowledge and learning.

Most importantly, all leaders within a renewed organization must communicate constantly. This should be done in a manner that is not only *ASAP*—As Soon As Possible—but also *AMAP*—As Much As Possible. All leaders in the renewed organization must make their own decisions or decisions will be made for them by contentious staff members. Leaders must be visible, and they have to enact a styled leadership easily recognizable by all organizational constituents, or fear will surely permeate the institution. Finally, all leaders within the renewed organization have a distinct responsibility to act as mentors, teachers, and facilitators during the process. These four responsibilities must be filled competently by all leaders in the renewed organization.

Strategic Initiatives

There are prominent factors, easily identifiable by healthcare leadership, that mandate a need to reorganize. A healthcare executive, along with the assistance and knowledge of managers, as well as with the input and experience of staff members, can scrutinize all of these mandates, and consider their resolution as the essential component of the reorganization plan.

Fiscal Conditions

The first reorganization mandate is the healthcare organization's current fiscal and market condition. The status of the organization relative to its customer/patient constituency, opportunity for growth within its market area, and current and future competition should be considered. If the organization, for example, has not enjoyed any considerable increased market growth or business progress, a remodeling of the organization is essential for basic survival. If, to use another example, the institution has made gains in a particular market—for example, the provision of mental health services—then the organization should be reconstructed in a manner that facilitates additional provision of these services.

This review of the organization's market and business condition should focus on the future, not the past or the present. With the emergence of single-parent and dual-income families, and other sociological change over the past twenty years, the customer/patient is demanding new and additional healthcare services. In order for a healthcare organization to succeed, it must be reconstructed in such a manner that it meets the community's current as well as future demands.

A good starting point is to review with staff a list of services the healthcare institution provides. In reviewing this list, the manager should not only discuss the staff's perceptions, opinions, and suggestions, but also those put forth by their neighbors and friends within the community. This type of feedback and input is unvarnished, motivated purely by community need, and not elicited by a questionnaire. Additionally, because the staff member belongs to the community (most healthcare employees live within a thirty-minute drive of their facility), he or she is a natural wellspring of information and input the organization can use to restructure. The employee can offer further insight into the community's perceived need for additional services, or for services that address some of the new maladies affecting the typical American healthcare consumer.

Staff Underutilization

A second major mandate for rightsizing, restructuring, and renewing a healthcare organization is staff underutilization. It is startling that in many healthcare organizations, based on the author's consulting experience, staff members are not fully utilized. In many institutions, individuals who are well-motivated perform many responsibilities that are not reflected in their job description. Thus, an organization that uses job descriptions as a primary review tool in assessing performance is one that is doomed to failure. As a starting point, each manager within the organization should review each reporting position, using the matrix of responsibilities displayed in Figure 1.3, to ensure that all employees are being utilized at full capacity. By not only employing the job description as a review tool, but by asking the employee to add additional job components in the appropriate column—as indicated in Figure 1.3—an overall perspective of total staff utilization can be realized.

Obviously, positions that are not fully utilized should either be eliminated or combined. But reviewing staff utilization can have other benefits. Staff underutilization exists in organizations where jobs have not been enhanced, position responsibilities have not been enriched, or institutions have simply become "creatures of habit." That is, individuals have not been motivated toward redefining their job positions and have not made additional contributions through their job. A review of staff utilization could motivate staff members to "prove their worth" to the organization. Also, the review could identify some areas that could benefit from restructuring. Most importantly, it could indicate to staff and managers alike the need to renew and remodel the organization.

For example, if most employees are underutilized in a particular section, it might be that the service has become outmoded. On the other hand, if several employees within a section can indicate that they are working at "120 percent" capacity, then this section might need bolstering through additional personnel. This segment might also be the first target for reorganization. By examining individual staff utilization, and then looking at total staff utilization across departmental and division lines, the healthcare organization can determine its relative need for remodeling and reorganizing, and have an excellent starting point for beginning the process.

Loss of Productivity

Another reorganization mandate is that of loss of productivity. This of course is related directly to staff underutilization and is usually indicated by four quantitative measures:

1. Numerical indicators, which indicate for example the number of operations performed by a medical surgery area, the number of individuals admitted to a particular section of the hospital, or the number of procedures that are performed by a particular department.
2. Percentage indicators, which might indicate quantitative trends in terms of a loss percentage of effectiveness, a drop in the percentage

Figure 1.3 Job Component Analysis Worksheet

Job Responsibility	Time Quotient	Weighted Value	Performance Value
PERFORMANCE VALUE WORKSHEET			
Position			
1			
2			
3			
4			
5			
6			
7			
8			
9			
10			
TOTALS			

of individuals using a particular segment of the organization, or a drop in the percentage of admissions in an inpatient area.

3. Cost indicators, which represent lost revenue in a particular area, for example, or an increase of revenue and profitability in another, emergent area.

4. Time indicators, which indicate the amount of time an employee might spend on a particular process, or areas in which the employee spends a considerable amount of time productively on behalf of the organization and of distinct benefit to the customer/patient.

These indicators are vital not only in their diagnostic worth in reorganizing the healthcare organization, but they also are good "teaching tools" for explaining to employees the need to reorganize and restructure the organization. Healthcare workers are instinctively knowledgeable of quantitative indicators, and these indicators can prove a point better than mere anecdotal evidence. In addition to proving that reorganization is vital, these mandates can also help the employees recognize how reorganization will affect their job position.

The primary quantitative factor is that of the census of the entire healthcare organization. If census numbers are not high, most staff members are sure to recognize the need for reorganization. In fact, fear often exists in a healthcare organization where leadership does not take swift, decisive action to correct a "dip in the census." Not addressing low census numbers can lead to the employees' loss of confidence in the institution and a resultant lack of commitment to their individual professional responsibilities.

Low census numbers can also extend to individual departments and services. As already noted, a hospital that is enjoying increased utilization of outpatient areas should facilitate the outpatient process and reconstruct its organization to accommodate the increased consumer demand for those services. This shift might prove to be devastating for the inpatient areas of the organization but, if done sensitively and ethically, can actually preserve jobs in the process. For example, a dietary worker who works specifically with inpatients can, with the help of training and reeducation, learn how to serve outpatients, working perhaps in the cafeteria or extended meal programs, or supporting a home health care agency operating under the corporate umbrella of the employing hospital. The more forthright an organization is in understanding and addressing census indicators, the greater likelihood that it will reach a fair, humane solution to resolve the problems presented by a shift in census numbers.

Salaries and Compensation

Less obvious, though still a relevant mandate, is a shift in compensation trends. For example, if a particular group of professionals has not received a significant pay raise, due to a lack of "market value" increases, it is very likely that that particular group is not in high demand. This is usually because their services are not being used as often as they were in previous years. On the other hand, if certain professionals have seen a dramatic increase in their market value—certain types of nursing, for example—this is a strong indicator that customer/patients value these services and that the employing organization might consider a renewed organizational model that provides these services in a greater abundance.

For example, a community hospital in southern New Jersey has recognized that mental health maintenance is a major product for its community. Accordingly, mental health professionals have enjoyed an increase in compensation, not only because of their market worth within the community but due to revenue they generate. As a result, this particular hospital has thrived by shifting the focus of its caregiving strategy to providing mental health services while decreasing—at an appropriate rate—other services.

Hiring Patterns

Other underlying reorganization mandates are hiring patterns and attrition rates within the facility. For example, if few individuals have been employed by a new department, due to a lack of demand for increased professionals, it is very possible that there is a decreased demand for these services. Similarly, if positions have not been filled in a particular area of the hospital—within the radiology department, for example—and there has been no loss of productivity, the organization should make the smart decision to eliminate the position entirely. This is premised on the fact that customer/patients are probably receiving radiological services from another community competitor, or possibly work is being performed more efficiently in the department in question: Perhaps the radiology department is using MRIs instead of standard x-ray machines, for example, thus obviating the need for an x-ray technician.

When a position opens because of attrition or promotion, the organization should use the matrix displayed in Figure 1.3 to determine if indeed a new employee should be hired. Additionally, the first move in rightsizing an organization should be to freeze all open positions and ensure that existing members are working at full capacity. As a reorganization mandate, currently open positions should be scrutinized fully to ensure that the service provided by the position is needed.

Fear

The element of fear can never be underestimated during the renewal process. Fear is prominent in healthcare organizations that are undergoing change—which is essentially every healthcare facility in the United States and Canada. Fear manifests itself primarily through poor morale across organizational lines and by the reluctance of staff members to:

- try something new;
- be creative in their jobs;
- attend organizational functions; or
- vary their performance from the prescripts of the job description.

Fear also causes employees to:

- openly question the organization;
- openly express fear that the organization will survive; or
- remain constantly pessimistic about the future of the organization.

Although they can be caused by a poorly handled reorganization effort, these factors—as well as an assortment of other emotional reactions—can be present in an organization that has not yet begun—and is in desperate need of—such an effort.

In reorganizing the organization, with a sense of renewing the healthcare facility's mission, primary objective, and commitment to the community, a strong message can be sent to all those who have a stake in the organization—employees, the community, and management—that the institution has redirected itself to be on "the right track for the future."

All of these reorganization mandates must be assessed—with the full participation of all organizational members—and they should be discussed frankly as the central points for the renewed organization and new organizational model. As we will see throughout this book, the more participation elicited from staff members throughout the reorganization process, the greater the chance that the process will become successful and positive for the organization's long-term growth and progress.

Positive Outcomes of Reorganization

Throughout the process, leadership at every level of the healthcare institution must reinforce the positive outcomes of reorganization, because it can frighten even the best performers in a healthcare institution. Accordingly, before the reconstruction process takes place, fifteen benefits of reorganization should be emphasized to all employees.

1. **Organizational survival.** For a healthcare organization to survive, it must adjust its basic efforts, mission, and intent to the needs of its most important stakeholder—the customer/patient. This should be the guiding beacon during the reconstruction process and should be supported by every member of the organization. Furthermore, the organization should seek not only to survive, but to thrive. The renewed model of the organization should perfectly reflect its values, mission, and overall intent in meeting the present and future needs of its customer constituency.

2. **Future readiness.** The renewed healthcare organization must be ready to meet its future needs, inasmuch as those needs can be predicted on present trends. The organization must ensure that the renewed organizational model results in an entity that is able to adapt to the needs of the future, perceptive and communicative in understanding future customer/patient needs, and professional in providing all services that will be needed in the future.

3. **Community commitment.** The reconstruction of a healthcare facility indicates to its customer community that it is not immune from rightsizing. Like all other community entities, the healthcare organization acknowledges its responsibility to be effective and efficient in scope and direction by reconstructing itself, redefining its mission, and reestablishing its basic commitment to the community. If presented properly to the constituent community, this remodeling presents a wonderful opportunity to reenergize an organization's commitment to itself, as well as to reestablish trust between the community and the organization, as we will see throughout this book.

4. **Performance maximization.** The well-worn cliché "lean and mean" is perhaps the most useful way to define performance maximization. In the renewed healthcare organization, great performers are given the opportunity to excel, to create new ways to address customer/patient needs and concerns, and to thrive on the change and renewed organizational commitment that renewal will bring. These employees will also be given the opportunity to help contribute to their organization's stability—as well as to their own basic job security—by contributing fully to the institution and utilizing their talents fully. For individual members who are not particularly committed to their healthcare facility, a renewed organizational initiative gives them the opportunity to decide, as adults and professionals, whether they want to be part of the new organization. At all three levels of performers—the "superstar," the "steady" player, and

the contentious "nonplayer"—the opportunity to perform at a maximum level should be stressed.

5. **Maintaining fiscal responsibility.** Another positive outcome of reorganization is a commitment to fiscal responsibility. As the organization reconstructs itself, every opportunity should be given toward presenting cost-efficient, quality-conscious solutions to pressing caregiving problems. The provision of services should be increased, while allowing for cost savings whenever possible. However, while fiscal pressure—as we have discussed—is most typically seen as the reason for rightsizing, it must be kept in mind that it is only a symptom and not the illness. Accordingly, one of the positive benefits of reorganization should be maintaining fiscal responsibility, but not at the expense of quality of care or other important initiatives, such as service, commitment, and compassion.

6. **Organizational galvanization.** Just as rubber and other synthetic compounds must be galvanized—that is, blended together for a tighter, cohesive structure—one of the underlying benefits of organizational restructuring is the galvanization of the institution. Put bluntly, the survivors of organizational rightsizing are usually very appreciative of the fact that they still have jobs—provided that the organization fully discloses that the rightsizing "cut" is well measured and others will not occur. As a result, interdepartmental cooperation often escalates, and individual interdependence usually increases as a direct result of the realization that in order to do more with less, "nobody wins unless we all win" in an organization.

Furthermore, a third bromide could be added—sometimes, "addition by subtraction" can be beneficial to a healthcare organization.

7. **Opportunity to redirect.** The renewed organization should end up with a new organizational charter, credo, and set of objectives. During the change process, however, the healthcare executive has a tremendous opportunity to send one of two messages about organizational redirection. First, the executive can state, given the current times of change and chaos, that the organization must redirect itself and remodel its structure in order to thrive in these new times. Second, the senior executive, particularly if he or she is new, can state that the organization was not particularly on "the right track" and the renewal, along with its attendant reconstruction, is necessary to get on the right one.

In either case, the promise of a renewed organization provides an opportunity for the CEO to generate a sense of enthusiasm for the new direction of the healthcare institution.

8. **Optimization of resources**. If an organization renews itself properly, it can expect to optimize its resources fully. While this certainly includes fiscal resources, the renewed facility will be able to use the talents of those individuals in the institution who are providing the majority of the work effort—an organization's operational resources—to meet the demands of the customer/patient more effectively. Organizational renewal can not only empower but encourage the strongest contributors in an organization to practice their craft, but it will also allow these performers the professional opportunity to grow and develop in their jobs while contributing optimally to the institution.

9. **Competitive edge**. The renewed organization can compete more effectively against others in its market. The facility that remodels itself according to the needs of the customer/patient community is logically the competitor who will be the preeminent provider of healthcare services in its market. Taken one step further, the organization that embraces the proper model for reconstruction is the one that will appear most "user friendly" to its customer/patient constituency. To this end, organizational reconstruction can provide the stellar healthcare organization with the opportunity to "get the jump" on its competitors.

10. **Social commitment**. The redefined healthcare organization demonstrates to its community a commitment to the current upheavals currently facing American society. The renewed organization addresses new maladies that heretofore were not addressed by the typical American hospital, such as AIDS and other physical and mental illnesses. The renewed institution meets the needs of the new American constituents, who are somewhat apprehensive and indeed fearful of healthcare provision and concerned about the very basic premise that healthcare might not be available—or at least affordable—to all American citizens. The renewed healthcare organization understands that it must be "lean and mean" and of the right size, just like its corporate counterparts, to maintain maximum credibility.

11. **Elimination of employee anxiety**. In short, healthcare employees are fearful. They are fearful of their job security, fearful of the future of American healthcare, fearful of both the increased negative scrutiny provided by the media and government, and fearful of a host of other factors. To combat this apprehension, the reorganization process forces staff members not to worry about things they cannot control, but instead to contribute to things that they can. Principally, what the individual staff member can control is his or her contribution—through communication, input, and, most importantly, action—to the new organizational model. The staff member can participate, rather than observe, the process.

Therefore, the individual staff member's anxiety will be eased by the effort that is put forth in contributing to the renewed organization.

12. **Elimination of employee emotionalism.** As has been discussed, people become fearful when faced with change. Healthcare organizations today—all of whom are facing change in one form or another—have staff members who react to this fear with contention, negativism, and a host of other emotions that prevent effective delivery of healthcare services. Therefore, a healthcare organization that undertakes a renewal, reorganization, and redirection initiative is one that will foster a sense of strength by addressing the change that is causing fear. The renewed institution will eliminate the negative emotionalism, as opposed to organizations where "nothing is done," or the premise of "we've always done it that way" is the rule of the day. Most healthcare organizational members are savvy enough to know that no institution is insulated from change, and that insular thinking can result in the demise of the organization. As employees recognize this, renewal can become a major catalyst in shifting organizational emotionalism from negative to positive.

13. **Introduction of a New Era.** Given the impression shared by most organizational members that something "new and different" must be done to meet current challenges, the healthcare executive must ensure that a balance is struck between Bill Gates and Florence Nightingale— that is, between business and the sacred mission of healthcare. A renewed organization takes into account many business dynamics; new organizational practices; and a spectrum of creative, progressive business approaches. However, the New Era must not lose in its enthusiasm the basic precepts of the healthcare organization:

- The customer/patient is at the top of the organizational chart.
- Compassion and dignity are time-honored traditions.
- Although a business, we are essentially a human service.
- We are the community public trust for healthcare in our area.
- Change is not made for the sake of change; change takes place to make us better so that we can do our job better.
- Our job is perhaps the most important job of all: taking care of people who need our services in times of ill health and during life-or-death situations.

A New Era for a healthcare organization can indeed be exciting and can help establish new directions for the institution's mission, direction, and focus. However, all of these attributes of the New Era must be underscored forcibly and visibly by an allegiance to the basic mission of the healthcare institution as a community trust.

14. **Sending appropriate messages.** One of the major benefits of healthcare organizational renewal is that it sends the appropriate messages to constituents. Healthcare renewal indicates to the customer/patients that their voices have been heard and a new model has been enacted to meet their needs more efficiently and effectively. Renewal also sends a message to employees that participants and individuals who are committed to organizational growth and progress will be rewarded. It further reminds contentious and self-serving individuals that their performance must be more selfless, productive, and motivated.

It is important to note that every stakeholder in the healthcare organizational scheme will interpret renewal differently. There must be a clarity, therefore, in the message sent by the organization's leadership. The message should encompass these points:

- Renewal is taking place to meet the demands of the customer/patient.
- Renewal is taking place to meet the demands of the future.
- Renewal is taking place to help increase the organization's efficiency and effectiveness.
- Renewal is taking place to help increase the odds for stability and progressive security in the future.
- Renewal is taking place to challenge and inspire all members of the organization toward peak performance.

By considering these tenets when communicating during the reorganization process, the healthcare organization takes a proactive approach toward getting the right message out to all stakeholders.

15. **Public relations and community relations value.** As implied in the previous point, the entire community interprets the organization's renewal differently. Therefore, the cosmetics of reconstruction are as important as the reconstruction itself, as perception is often as important as reality. For example, many of the author's clients have adopted for their institution a new color scheme, a new credo, or a new advertising "tag line" that not only celebrates the renewal but reinforces the traditions and lore of the particular healthcare institution. As we will see throughout this book, there are several strategies that the reader can use to realize the full public relations value of an organization's renewal and reconstruction.

Stewardship Responsibilities

Throughout this book, there are many practical approaches—such as those already featured in this first chapter—that can be used immediately by the reader. Essentially, the role of a leader through the entire reorganization process is to act with a sense of stewardship in implementing the renewal strategy. The leader must demonstrate a certain amount of decency and indicate what is right and wrong as reorganization takes place. The leader must also demonstrate a sense of fortitude, and take a stand whenever appropriate in the interest of the organization and its patients. The leader must be industrious and demonstrate visibly—through hard work and direct contribution—that a distinctly higher work ethic is needed in the renewed organization in order for it to be successful. Likewise, the leader must demonstrate a sense of integrity, support the decisions made by subordinates, be honest and candid in all responses to questions, and maintain confidentiality whenever needed.

Part of the stewardship responsibilities of the healthcare leader in the reorganization process, particularly during the initial stages, is to promulgate knowledge. As has been mentioned throughout this chapter, it is essential to use the points delineated here to communicate not only *how* change will take place, but *why* it must take place. More importantly, these points should be used for discussions and conversations in which the individual staff member is provided the opportunity to present specific solutions and suggestions that might abet the reorganization process.

Community commitment must also be part of the stewardship responsibility, and this will become apparent throughout this book, particularly when specific strategies such as rightsizing and managerial action are examined. Furthermore, the organization must maintain a sense of fidelity to both the community and other stakeholders throughout the reorganization process, as demonstrated by an increase in service effectiveness and the introduction of new medical services, among other positive benefits facilitated by renewal and reconstruction.

Social awareness should be paramount in the stewardship scheme. Like a ship's captain, who is always watchful of changing environmental conditions when piloting his or her ship, the executive should look at environmental factors such as customer perception, prevailing medical needs, and current trends that might determine the future course for the renewed organization. The executive must also use resources optimally and recognize that there are no ideas to waste, no solutions that do not merit consideration, and no member of the organization who can afford to be a passive spectator rather than an active participant in the reorganization process. Finally, the inspiration of allegiance and loyalty throughout the entire process, as we will see throughout the book, is a defining element in whether renewal and reconstruction can succeed.

2

FORMING A STRATEGIC PLAN

Forming a solid plan to rightsize, reconstruct, and renew a healthcare organization is perhaps the most critical step in the entire reorganization process. The direction an organization will take depends on its ability to rightsize itself effectively, taking into account personnel staffing levels, a reconstruction plan that will better serve the customer/patient, and development of renewal processes that will enhance morale, professional dedication, and future action. Without such a concrete plan, the reorganization process can easily go awry. Furthermore, without due consideration of these and many other factors, many minor considerations can turn into major stumbling blocks during the change process.

In this chapter, we will review what must be considered during reorganization and examine the overriding factor that affects the whole renewal process—fear. Additionally, we will look at the essential dynamics of change, as well as how managerial and executive power and influence must be exerted in order to make the process a successful one. Furthermore, we will review the specific benefits of rightsizing, reconstruction, and renewal and discuss how these benefits can be communicated to the entire organization.

Understanding and Resolving the "Fear Factor"

Any restructuring healthcare organization will suffer a barrage of rumors and conjecture about the process, even before it begins. This problem is rooted in the "rumor mill" that exists at every hospital or healthcare institution. Furthermore, because nearly every industry is undergoing some form of downsizing, individuals working at healthcare organizations will naturally expect that rightsizing will eventually affect their institution. Accordingly, as soon as a census report indicates a decrease in a hospital's inpatient population, employees will naturally believe that rightsizing will follow. This of course will cause fear among the employees.

It is important for the healthcare leader to understand how fear manifests itself among the staff; furthermore the leader must address that fear. Fundamentally, there are two types of fear that exist in healthcare facilities undergoing reorganization. The first is general fear, which relates to all staff members. The second type is performance-specific fear, which is illustrated in Figure 2.1.

Fear of Job Loss

The first element of general fear relates to loss of employment. Most individuals in an organization with a decreasing census and declining revenue are concerned about their job security. Individuals who work in healthcare are extremely observant, perceptive, and attuned to most business dynamics. They therefore instinctively recognize that reorganization might take place, and, as a result, their job security might be threatened. Potential loss of employment is certainly an understandable and realistic concern for any individual.

Once fear of job loss takes root in an organization, the staff's morale, individual motivation, and attention to critical details are quickly abandoned in favor of self-preservation and justifiable self-interest. That is, employees begin to question the value of being dedicated if their job might not exist after the reorganization process. This doubt can obviously lead to an erosion of care, quality, and patient service throughout the organization.

But any practical reorganization process requires a review of every position in the institution. Thus, the organizations must undertake a

Figure 2.1 Performance-Specific Fears

Negative Sentiments	Positive Countermeasures
False Information	Fortitude
Employment Reduction or Loss	Effectiveness and Efficiency
Anarchy and Apprehension	Affiliation
Regression	Recognition

position review analysis process. In this process, each position within the organization would be evaluated relative to:

1. **Performance.** The specific components of each job must be analyzed to determine its critical contributions and significant action provided to the institution's mission: providing quality healthcare to the customer/patient.

2. **Potential.** The review must determine the position's potential to contribute to the organization in the near future. For example, an organization shifting from inpatient to outpatient services must examine each position to evaluate how it will contribute to a decentralized outpatient setting, as opposed to a traditional hospital inpatient setting.

3. **Progressive promise.** Each position should be evaluated to determine the long-term benefits he or she will provide the restructured organization.

The most important element of a position review analysis is the participation of all employees. Fundamentally, employees should be asked how they will contribute to their position, the potential of their position for the new organization, and the promise their position holds for the long-term future of the organization. During this exercise, it is essential that the institution provide a general perception of what the renewed organization will look like and at least its basic objectives. Employees can then justify the value of their position as the reorganization process takes place. Using a position analysis matrix, completed with the assistance of a unit manager or supervisor, or simply updating the job descriptions, can complete this objective as an accurate, current depiction of performance and contribution is constructed.

Employee participation in this exercise helps assuage the fear caused by rightsizing. However, the organization bears an additional responsibility: It must promise that individuals and personalities will not be considered during the rightsizing efforts. That is, the essential appraisal will be job positions and specific technical contributions. In many organizations, rightsizing has become disastrous when the essential determining factor for retaining job positions has been based on personality, or worse, tenure. While it is quite easy merely to dismiss the individuals who have been with the organization the shortest time, a great deal of technical talent and dedicated personnel can be lost, while more long-term, "backwards-thinking" individuals are retained. By analyzing each job position with the participation of the employee, the institution can make a more intelligent choice about its reorganization.

Another general fear is that of organizational survival. When an institution is confronted with the specter of rightsizing, the rumor mill will almost certainly point to the possibility of acquisition, merger, alliance, or in extreme cases, organizational demise. These rumors will no doubt be spread by the individuals cited as "nonplayers" in Figure 2.2.

Of course, in some cases, a merger or a new alliance might be, in fact, part of the reconstruction effort. If this occurs, individuals at every level of the organization will once again speculate on their job security. In this case, management must once again conduct a position analysis process. This should take place at every level of the new organization, specifically in cases of mergers where two individuals in two separate hospitals might conduct the same basic job duties.

Communication becomes the key to success. As soon as the chief executive of an organization is certain that a merger, acquisition, or alliance is imminent, appropriate information should be given to all members of the organization. This is further illustrated in the case study in Chapter 8. The executive should be honest in explaining that while jobs will be preserved, a streamlining might take place in which jobs and departments are combined. However, all of this information should be prefaced by the executive's commitment to review each job position and performance based on merit and value to the organization and the customer/patient, rather than implement a "quick fix" approach, in which positions will be combined based merely on title and basic job description.

Performance-Specific Fear

As we have stated, the second type of fear is performance-specific fear. As indicated in Figure 2.2, healthcare professionals essentially perform

Figure 2.2 Organizational Performance Categories

Performers and Characteristics	Percentage of Organizational Composition	How Reorganization Frightens Them
	Superstars	
• Stellar Performance • Thrive on Challenge • Define the System	15–20%	• Loss of Opportunities • Regression • Loss of Competitive Edge
	Steady/Strong Players	
• Satisfactory Performance • Strive to Succeed • Support the System	60–70%	• Loss of Job Security • Loss of Stability • Loss of Future Focus
	Nonplayers	
• Questionable Performance • Self-Centered • Eradicate the System	10–15%	• Increased Workload • New Tasks • Job Expansion

at three basic levels. As a result, their performance-specific fear is related to their relative performance level and must be addressed as such.

The "Superstar"

The "superstar" healthcare professional is someone who personifies excellent performance, the strong values of the organization, and a distinct commitment to perform "above and beyond" job expectations. These individuals usually act as charismatic leaders throughout the organization, and are seen as role models by their peers and, if they are managers, their subordinates. However, fear of rightsizing will no doubt permeate their professional perceptions during reorganization. The performance-related fear of the "superstar" healthcare professional is that he or she will be asked to assume tasks, job duties, and other work activities that are mundane, repetitive, and static. To the "superstar" performer who thrives on change, this is distasteful at best and demotivating at worst.

To combat this potentially negative dimension, the manager of a "superstar" employee should make a special effort to give him or her a set of responsibilities that will keep them fully engaged throughout the transition process. The easiest way to accomplish this is simply to ask the "superstar" to set forth a six-month action plan relative to his or her particular position, as it will be affected by the reorganization effort. "Superstar" employees are experts on how they can best contribute to the organization, and they can easily generate a set of objectives that would be pertinent, contributory, and beneficial. Over the course of six months, for example, a "superstar" in a pharmacy department can innovate a more efficient way to order pharmaceuticals, which is better for an organization than if he or she simply filled an increased amount of prescriptions because of the loss of a downsized fellow employee. While the "superstar" in all likelihood will be asked to fill more prescriptions, using his or her expertise in the process of redefining the logistical management of the pharmacy will keep them engaged and motivated.

The "Steady" Employee

The increase of job responsibilities and productivity is a major concern of the "steady" employee, who is well motivated and vitally interested in the organization's survival and recognizes that he or she will be asked to "do more with less," to use the most worn cliché in healthcare management. While these individuals are motivated, and certainly understand the need to "do more with less," they have been asked over the past five years in most typical healthcare settings to do so. Therefore, they are at the end of their threshold for increased responsibility. Once a rightsizing effort is incorporated into their work environment, it is easy to understand why the "steady" employees will feel as though they are approaching their "breaking point."

The artful healthcare leader will make every attempt to dispel this fear by keeping close contact with the "steady" employee, not only throughout the rightsizing process but before it even begins to take place. This can be done by arranging exclusive meetings between the manager and each "steady" employee, in which these dimensions are discussed:

- the likely outcomes of rightsizing;
- an expression of confidence in the employee to meet additional job responsibilities; and
- an understanding on the part of the manager that the employee has contributed strongly in the past and will no doubt continue to maintain a strong level of performance.

During this meeting, the manager and the "steady" employee should discuss which additional resources could be used to reduce overwork, or at least ways to alleviate some of the additional job responsibilities.

Most importantly, the manager must explain clearly to the employee that any time is a good time to discuss any concern, question, or idea that might ease the transition process. A manager who takes an "ostrich approach" to rightsizing, specifically when dealing with a "steady" employee, is one who is doomed to failure. Most "steady" employees in a healthcare organization are motivated by the contribution that they make, job satisfaction, recognition, and the opportunity to be affiliated with a progressive healthcare institution. The manager must recognize that rightsizing will not be easy, that each "steady" employee is an expert on how to make the change more expedient, and that a joint effort must be made between the manager and the "steady" employee toward determining the best course of action during the reorganization effort. Constant, clear communication of these three objectives can dispel the "steady" employee's fear of rightsizing.

The "Nonplayer"

The bottom tier of performance is populated by the "nonplayers" of a healthcare organization. These individuals perform below expectations, are poorly motivated, have no allegiance to the organization, and usually behave counterproductively. They are classified by healthcare managers as being contentious, "high maintenance," passive/aggressive, and a number of other negative descriptions. The primary fear of "nonplayers" during rightsizing is that they will have to work harder. This blunt assessment requires some explanation.

In the past, healthcare organizations did not have to maintain an extraordinary interest in their "bottom line." Furthermore, management development was not as sophisticated in healthcare as in other industries, nor was it available to all managers on a timely basis. As a result, certain individuals who did not perform at a particularly high level were retained by a healthcare organization, both because their performance evaluations were poorly done and, frankly, because the organization could afford to retain them. Unfortunately, over time, these individuals became long-term employees, replete with good performance evaluations, regular pay increases, and other benefits that should have been reserved for the "steady" employees.

As an organization seeks to rightsize, these individuals are relatively well entrenched. It is difficult, if not impossible in some cases, to remove them from the organization during the process. However, every accountable healthcare organization undergoing a restructuring effort should take every opportunity possible to remove these individuals. This can be done in a number of ways. First, by conducting a position review analysis, it will become the responsibility of the "nonplayer" to justify the existence of his or her job. If the "nonplayer" uses his or her job description solely to justify their position, the analysis will invariably come up short with regard to future potential, promise, and performance. In some cases, a "nonplayer" can be eliminated if their sector of the business is deemed to be nonviable. For example, the author recently consulted on a major reorganization process at a New England hospital in which there were separate departments of social work, clinical psychology, and psychiatry. Each of these departments was only working at 30 percent capacity. By combining the three departments, and making every effort to redesign this new mental health unit, "nonplayers" were naturally eliminated, as the new unit acquired a higher level of acumen, future potential, and performance qualifications from each of its members. The "nonplayers" who had fallen behind their respective fields, had not achieved any new credentials, and had contributed to the loss of business within their departments were objectively eliminated.

However, this example is unfortunately more often the exception than the rule. It can be legally perilous to eliminate a "nonplayer" who, for example, has seventeen years of experience with the organization with "meets expectations" performance evaluations. Moreover, the fear of "having to do more work" is not an acceptable fear, especially in a healthcare organization. Therefore, when dealing with the "nonplayer," the manager should use fear as a motivating factor. The best way to do so is for the manager to draw a redefined set of objectives for the "nonplayer" just as would be done for the "steady" and "superstar" employees. This should be done immediately, well before the beginning of the formal rightsizing process. In many cases, the "nonplayer," confronted with the possibility of having to do considerably more work, will either resign, look for work elsewhere, or perhaps take early retirement.

When a "nonplayer" leaves an organization during this time, it can best be typified as "healthy attrition." All healthcare organizations must recognize that their basic survival is threatened by the "nonplayer." They must also realize that the nefarious effect of the "nonplayer" on the institution is heightened during times of drastic change—specifically during rightsizing. The most efficient way of dealing with the "nonplayer" is to address that he or she will indeed have to do more work during the rightsizing, reconstruction, and renewal process. If the manager uses the performance evaluation process, the job description process, and other human resource management techniques to set higher standards fairly and distinctly, "nonplayers" will have to decide whether they will be suited for the new organization.

"Nonplayers" will fight the renewal process every step of the way, from the rightsizing to the reorganization. Throughout, "nonplayers" will complain, question, negate, and subjugate any attempt at change. In the appendix, "Managing Nonplayer Resistance to Change," there are twenty excuses given by "nonplayers," the basic psychology and rationale of these excuses, and the best ways to answer them. Healthcare leaders must be aware of the activities of any "nonplayers" on their staff. They must also realize that—if unchecked—these employees can inflict a great amount of damage to the healthcare institution and, by extension, to the customer/patient.

"House Rules"

For all three types of performers within a healthcare organization, basic stress-related fears exist. Personal stress can exist with all employees who are asked to "do more with less." Organizational stress will certainly be exhibited throughout the entire process, and, as we shall see, the renewal process can help ameliorate it. Community stress can be evident in some cases, as community members worry about their healthcare institution during times of change. Once again, however, the renewal process can help address this, as we will see in later chapters.

Community-based stress can increase if rumors are allowed to spread through the community. Therefore, an organization should institute a set of five basic rules that are clear, ethical, and enforceable. Not following these "house rules" will result in immediate termination. These five are:

1. What we discuss about the reorganization effort must stay in the hospital. Our plans must not be released to community members who are not employed by the hospital.
2. The executive management of the organization is responsible for external communication—not the employees.
3. Any communication from the community that has been collected by employees—and that might be beneficial—should be shared with the organization.
4. Any ideas about how we can communicate to the community about our new plans *at the right time* will be welcomed.
5. The overriding motivation for our reconstruction process is the customer/patient. Therefore, deliberately generating rumors and other types of "fear-mongering" by any staff member will not be tolerated under any conditions.

While this will not curtail the predilection of "nonplayers" for disseminating rumors and other types of information to community members, it at least puts them on notice that this is unacceptable behavior. Furthermore, in its worst form, disseminating false information about a healthcare institution to a community member by a "nonplayer" is a legal offense. The organization should take this opportunity to rid itself of that offending employee.

Interpersonal stress and patient-related stress are the two final components of the fear factor. In hospitals undergoing rightsizing, patients are naturally concerned about the type of care they receive—and they may be worried that it will be substandard. This fear also extends itself to interpersonal relationships among staff members, who wonder if they will get the same support, collegiality, and input from their peers and supervisors during the change process. To this end, an extra set of "house rules" should be instituted:

1. Take the "extra step" when dealing with all patients. For example, if an individual asks for directions to Ward 4, do not merely tell them how to get to Ward 4, walk them there.
2. Promise people answers. The worst thing a healthcare professional can say to a patient during rightsizing is, "I don't know." If you cannot answer a question immediately, promise the person an answer and tell them precisely when you will have it.
3. Never say, "It's not my job." This plays to the biggest fear of the customer/patient—that is, the person whose job it is to take care of me is being rightsized! Immediately make every effort to facilitate a meeting between the patient and the respective professional within the healthcare organization who can render the care the patient is seeking.

4. Any time is a good time for a question, idea, or suggestion on how we can better serve the patient.

5. Any time is a good time for an idea, suggestion, or better way of serving each other.

6. Any time is a good time to ask for assistance. Under no condition should anyone within an organization feel uncomfortable when asking a colleague for additional assistance or support.

By recognizing the fear factors within a healthcare organization during the change process—specifically during rightsizing—the healthcare leader can systematically address these fears, and, more importantly, resolve potential performance problems before they occur.

"Making the Cut"

At the core of any reorganization strategy—especially the rightsizing effort—is determining which services, departments, or individuals to eliminate. This is a professional challenge to the executive and can be personally traumatic. In essence, the organization's executive cadre must balance the need to stay fiscally responsible and operationally efficient with the unfortunate circumstance of eliminating job positions—and in doing so, affecting the livelihood of many employees.

In this section, we will define the essential dynamics of reorganization and rightsizing. These dynamics apply to all three elements of reorganization—rightsizing, reconstruction, and renewal—but in this introduction, we will explore each one of these dynamics as it relates specifically to the rightsizing dimension of "making the cut." For a reorganization to succeed, all fourteen of the characteristics, as illustrated in Figure 2.3, must be present in all three phases of the reorganization effort.

A Humane Approach

First, all reorganization efforts must be humane. The healthcare executive must be acutely aware throughout the reorganization process that

Figure 2.3 Essential Characteristics of Reorganization

- Humane Approach
- Value Driven
- Stakeholder Driven
- Technically Solid
- Business Based
- Future Focused
- Progressively Managed
- Legally Sound
- Community Centered
- Comprehensively Communicated
- "Top-Down, Management-First"
- Effective and Efficient
- Resources Positive
- Mutually Beneficial

employees' lives will be drastically affected. This thought, however, must share equal consideration with the life and health of the customer/patient. A balance must be struck between these two considerations, for in many ways they are inseparable. For example, most healthcare employees belong to the community in which they work, and, in essence, are not only employees, but also patients. Furthermore, community members who do not work at the healthcare organization certainly are friends and neighbors to many individuals who do and are thus personally affected by any rightsizing action.

Regarding reconstruction and renewal, humanistic considerations— as we will see later in this book—are applied easily, especially when considering the individual dignity and professional productivity of employees of the renewed organization. When rightsizing, however, an organization wishing to appear humane and sensitive to employee needs must incorporate these dimensions:

- All individuals eligible for retirement, and even early retirement, are to be given prompt consideration and the opportunity to take it. An often overlooked strategy in many rightsizing efforts, this is not only fiscally intelligent but also humanistically oriented, as it provides a unique reward for long-term employees who have contributed consistently to the organization.
- The organization should make every effort to retain services that have a high visibility throughout the community, such as an AIDS clinic or an acute care facility.
- The organization must maintain services that historically have been valued by the community, such as maternity and pediatrics, despite their potential for poor financial return.
- The organization has to emphasize that there are many more reasons for change than just fiscal austerity, and all of these reasons together will lead to better future services for the community.
- The organization should in fact deemphasize financial considerations in the rightsizing effort, treating such concerns as "necessary evils," not part of the overall process.
- The organization must emphasize that the reorganization is taking place to better serve the patient, and as a result, rightsizing must occur. However, rightsizing is occurring as part of an overall process, not as a direct result of a reconstruction effort. In other words, an organization is not "rightsizing" and terminating employment merely to move to a new model, such as a product-line organizational model. Rather, it is taking place to facilitate a reconstruction, which will then lead to a renewal, whose ultimate end is to take better care of the customer/patient.

- Input has to be sought and suggestions elicited from the employees about making the reorganization process a viable, progressive, constructive one.
- Specific consideration must be given to employees who have demonstrated a strong, "superstar" level of performance in one area that might be eliminated, and they should be given every opportunity possible to gain employment in other areas of the organization.
- Cuts in employment are based on progress, performance, and potential, and not merely tenure, personality, and the implicit threat of "nonplayer" retribution. That is, the needs of the customer/patient are the preeminent factor in deciding which services and employees will be retained, not personalities or vacuous threats of lawsuits, walkouts, and other negative "nonplayer" retribution.

The healthcare business is truly the "people business," and adherence to these guidelines is a first step toward ensuring that during reorganization, people come first.

Value

The entire reorganization, and notably the rightsizing effort, must be value driven, a term that has two meanings. First, the value that the organization provides to the customer/patient must be enhanced by the reorganization effort. Second, a set of ethical values should drive the entire process. Certain actions must take place that will assure all stakeholders of a healthcare organization that the reorganization effort in general, and the rightsizing effort in particular, is indeed value driven:

There can be no "special deals" for anyone in the organization. For example, if it is determined that a particular service is outmoded and five jobs must be eliminated, the organization must eliminate all five jobs. A "special deal" cannot be established for one member of the department simply because of personal needs, tenure, or other extrinsic characteristics.

Every attempt possible should be made to secure employment for displaced people. It is the particular responsibility of the human resources department during rightsizing to review all open positions, facilitate internal interviews, and seek to place "superstar" and "steady" employees in open positions elsewhere in the organization.

Every effort must be made to accommodate the special needs of any patient during the rightsizing effort. All patients must receive a consistent standard of decency, fairness, and respect.

The "cut" should be made quickly, resolutely, and with a high degree of closure. Perhaps the most unethical action that can be taken during rightsizing is to draw the process out unnecessarily, to let staff "linger" in their own stress while wondering who will be cut, and to exacerbate poor morale throughout a healthcare organization because of an unnecessary delay in conducting the actual rightsizing process.

Beginning with the rightsizing process, and continuing through to the renewal process, a new allegiance to the organization's values must be emphasized. Such qualities as decency, fortitude, industry, and integrity should be highlighted and celebrated whenever exhibited by employees. Other examples of this type of action and management reinforcement will be provided. At the beginning, however, it is important to remember that every leader in the healthcare organization during the rightsizing must show a sense of decency by listening and addressing the concerns and fears of all employees; a sense of fortitude by taking a cold, objective look at key positions; a sense of integrity by being honest with all peers, subordinates, and superiors; and a sense of industry by increasing their own managerial work efforts in the spirit of "doing more with less" on behalf of the customer/patient.

A healthcare organization's everyday actions always reflect its ethics. This becomes particularly true during times of crisis and rightsizing, and it is essential that all leaders of the organization understand that they are indeed "onstage" in the eyes of their employees and patients and must exhibit the four defining ethics—decency, fortitude, integrity, and industry—at every possible opportunity.

Stakeholders

The rightsizing effort must also be stakeholder driven. The interests of anyone who has a distinct investment in the rightsizing process, such as an employee, patient, or board member, must be taken into account. To this end, the following checklist reviews some important questions that must be considered when deciding what to cut:

- services that have demonstrated at least two years' worth of declining revenue or decreased utilization;
- services in which technology has been distinctly outmoded: for example, certain areas of radiology, laboratory services, and related technical fields;
- support services that have suffered a decline in utilization caused by a shift from inpatient services to outpatient services, such as food services and housekeeping;
- services that have been substantially replicated, if not duplicated, because of a merger or acquisition;
- services that have been both chronically underutilized by the patient community and will most likely be underutilized in the future;

- specific positions that are not being used to at least 70 percent capacity. Once again, the importance of position analysis exercises, which merely review the amount of job components coupled with a typical time quotient reflecting the percentage of time each day that the employee spends in that particular position, are extremely useful; and
- elements of the organization that the board of directors, executive management, and other critical decision makers have determined to be fiscally untenable or practically unrealistic to staff, manage, and fund in the near future.

The value of the component or position to the stakeholder must be the overriding consideration in determining what to cut. This should not only be the driving force but should be the overarching theme throughout the entire rightsizing process. That is, a leader must make clear, for the good of the patient we must move to a new type of organization.

Technology

The rightsizing effort must be technically sound. In this regard, there cannot be any gaps or errors in performance relative to the provision of technical support and services to the patient at any time, notably during reorganization. In order for a healthcare organization to appear to be technically sound, and in essence to *be* technically sound throughout the rightsizing process, the following regimen should be followed:

- All new technical innovations should be highlighted. It must also be explained how they work better and contribute to healthcare more efficiently than their outdated, outmoded predecessors.
- Any particular failures of the organization to address a technical issue, or to provide less-than-excellent care because of a technical gaffe, must be immediately corrected and the root cause of the error identified. If this is not done, most individuals in the organization will assume that the rightsizing effort caused a lack in care.
- Throughout the rightsizing process, individuals must be made aware of the fact that technological improvement in the healthcare sector has unfortunately displaced people from certain positions. This is clearly seen in areas such as ultrasound, nursing, and virtually any other patient care area. This is a fact of life in healthcare, and everyone in the organization must be made to recognize it as a reality.
- Managers should ask each member of their staff to list all of the technical innovations that have taken place in their particular technical field over the past five years. By completing this exercise, each individual will realize that the advances that have taken

place are indeed astounding and are a contributing factor to the reconstruction and renewal effort.

- In all cases, any benefits realized by the use of new technology *with* a new rightsizing scheme should be highlighted, publicized throughout the organization, and cited as evidence of the benefit of moving toward a "leaner, greener" facility.

If the organization does not exhibit the benefits of technology, staff will believe that technology is in fact replacing people. If a healthcare organization is perceived as allowing technology—read "machines"— to do this, it cannot rightfully expect to be seen as a "people-oriented institution."

Business

Reorganization and rightsizing efforts must also be business based. Most individuals who work in healthcare organizations recognize that healthcare is indeed both a business as well as a human service and seldom will quarrel with the notion that the organization must become more business-oriented in order to survive. However, a disproportionate focus on the business aspects of a healthcare organization at the expense of its humanistic service aspects can in fact poison its public perception, morale, and ultimately, its chances of survival.

Realistically, then, the best strategy is for the healthcare executive in the rightsizing organization to say, "We must do this if we want to stay in business." All but the most ardent of "nonplayers" will accept this as part of the rationale to reconstruct.

The following benefits of rightsizing and reorganization can be stressed by an astute healthcare leader:

- an immediate reduction of "red ink" resulting from the loss of rightsized personnel;
- a stronger profit-and-loss statement, as a direct result of the elimination of services that were redundant, outmoded, or underutilized;
- the perception of the customer community, as evidenced by letters, comments, and other stakeholder input, that the hospital has succeeded in making the "tough call" and has downsized in pace with the non-healthcare industrial community of its surrounding region;
- the added financial and operational resources available as a result of the rightsizing;
- the opportunity to meet the requisites of the hospital's annual budget, for example, due to the fiscal propriety of rightsizing; and

- the ability of the organization to enter into new, more progressive markets.

These business-based benefits can be coupled with the overriding organizational benefits of rightsizing, which appear at the end of this chapter, in order to provide the employee with a clearer, comprehensive picture of the business advantages of rightsizing and reorganization.

The Future

The rightsizing organization must focus on the future. The past is an unfortunate contrast to the current age of change in healthcare. Unfortunately, many individuals within a healthcare organization, specifically the "nonplayers," like to think the future will be just like the past. This is indeed foolhardy, given the change that has taken place in healthcare to date, not to mention the change that will no doubt occur in the next five years.

As a result, one of the overriding reasons for reorganization is to prepare for the future; managers should clearly detail these features:

- Reorganization will allow us to move into more progressive markets that will not only help us succeed in business but will allow us to provide newer services to our customer/patient.
- This will allow us in the future to become a "public trust" for all members of our community in need of healthcare services.
- It will also help us grow and prosper in the long run, whereas staying on course in our current incarnation will lead to failure, regression, and a lack of healthcare provision.
- Reorganization will give us a competitive advantage over other institutions that have not made the moves necessary to become forward-thinking healthcare organizations.
- Reorganization will help us to maintain in the future what has made us successful in the past—that is, being able to provide excellent service to the customer/patient. While somewhat painful in the short term, the entire reorganization effort will let us become the type of organization that will meet the needs of our patients ten years from now, not merely ten months from now.

By presenting these attributes in a realistic, nontheoretic fashion, most staff members will weigh their commitment to the institution with their desire to help contribute to a progressive organization that will provide employment, as well as good healthcare, in the future.

The entire reorganization process incorporates various features of rightsizing, then reconstruction, and then finally organizational renewal.

These processes must be progressively managed and sequentially over-seen from one phase to the next. In each phase, it is essential that all managers in the organization:

- clearly communicate any new information regarding any one of the three phases immediately, quickly, and comprehensively to all staff members;
- utilize "management by walking around," "management by coffee break," and any other "personal touch" management devices to stay informed about employee perception, sentiment, and communication;
- use crisis management and conflict management to manage resolutely any interdepartmental or interpersonal conflict that might arise because of changing work conditions resulting from the rightsizing effort;
- ask any and all appropriate questions to senior management regarding the conduct of the rightsizing effort;
- provide any pertinent information to senior management that might facilitate the rightsizing effort;
- courageously compose the rightsizing "lists"—that is, the list of individuals to be displaced—by objectively evaluating contribution to the organization;
- firmly manage "nonplayer" resistance throughout the rightsizing effort—including "rumor-busting," confronting "nonplayers," and making every possible effort to make the "nonplayers" part of the rightsized population;
- share experiences and episodes that might be instructive to others with their colleagues and peers during the rightsizing process, not just after as a "post-reduction" review after the process; and
- take whatever time necessary to discuss certain dimensions of the rightsizing process either collectively or individually with employees at any time necessary.

Throughout this book, we will present additional management strategies. However, adhering to these simple "rules of the road" from the outset of the process is extraordinarily helpful not only to the manager, but to the entire organization.

Legal and Ethical Considerations

Legal Concerns

The rightsizing process must be legally grounded. That is, every pertinent law must be followed.

However, a number of law firms take the unfortunate position of "minimal risk" when consulting healthcare organizations on rightsizing. These firms advocate the "cleanest" way of rightsizing, which usually is the easiest method and the one that leaves the least exposure for legal recourse. Unfortunately, this usually involves rightsizing only individuals with the least amount of tenure, while ensuring the jobs of those whose job positions might be underutilized or inappropriately fulfilled, and retaining individuals who have no true allegiance to the organization or any particular interest in performing at an exemplary level.

Ultimately, the question of who is eliminated from the organization—along with which services—becomes the decision of the chief executive and the executive cadre. These leaders must abide by whatever rightsizing decision is made, and ultimately it will affect their daily worklife as well as their overall healthcare career. Consequently, legal counsel should be taken as part of the decision-making process.

When "making the cut," legal counsel should be sought regarding:

- organized labor and union practices;
- unemployment, discrimination, and other worker rights issues;
- unlawful dismissal practices;
- the notification and reduction-in-force statutes; and
- potential class-action suits.

Although the legal aspects of rightsizing can be particularly damaging to an organization if mismanaged or inappropriately researched, rightsizing is so prevalent in American industry that cases where it has been legally challenged are far and few between. Accordingly, the healthcare organization that acts in the best interests of its patient, and follows the other guidelines explained in this section, will usually find itself on safe legal ground.

Community Perception

The rightsizing effort should be community centered, as should the reconstruction and renewal efforts. In order to involve the community proactively, these steps should be taken:

- Arrangements should be made with the local unemployment board and other related entities to help facilitate the processing of individuals who will be dismissed.
- Every effort should be made to arrange interviews and other appropriate pursuits of alternative employment throughout the community by the human resources department.

- Friendly relationships should be enhanced with the local media, and the communication to these various groups should be ongoing. (See the case study in Chapter 8 for additional details.)
- Local politicians should be notified and included at the appropriate time to provide appropriate counseling, reemployment, and community support.
- Members of the board of trustees and other prominent stakeholders who are involved should be used appropriately to communicate elements of the rightsizing process throughout the community in a professional, positive manner.
- Relevant nonprofit agencies who can assist in the rightsizing effort should be immediately enlisted.

Negative community perception of the rightsizing can result in devastating effects to the healthcare organization; community links should therefore be fully and proactively used to explain why it is both beneficial *and* necessary.

Intraorganizational Communication

The rightsizing effort must have at its root comprehensive communication. This becomes important not only in dealing with various community entities, as we have just discussed, but perhaps more importantly between managers and staff personnel throughout the healthcare organization. As soon as the decision is made to rightsize, these points should be communicated clearly by individual managers, with the support of the leadership, to all staff personnel:

- who is being rightsized;
- when the rightsizing will take place;
- the outplacement resources that will be given to the "rightsized" personnel;
- how the rightsizing will immediately affect each department;
- a reiteration of the benefits of the rightsizing;
- a request by managers to get as much input as possible from employees on how to make the rightsizing process as efficient and effective as possible;
- where the employee can go for additional counseling, if requested;
- a reaffirmation that the rightsizing will be a "one-time-only" endeavor and that no additional rightsizing is planned; and
- the organization's encouragement of retained employees to assist outplaced employees in any possible way.

Of course, all of these features must be modified according to confidentiality and circumstance. For example, in discussing *who* is being rightsized, the manager would probably not want to cite any specific names, but rather simply state that, "A few individuals in the radiology department were unfortunately affected by this rightsizing because of the scope of their job positions." Additionally, while the organization should encourage retained employees to assist outplaced employees in any regard, this would not extend itself to the notion of helping a few displaced "nonplayers" publicly vilify the organization.

In all cases, it is essential for the manager to err on the side of overcommunicating rather than undercommunicating. This obviously extends itself to the dimensions of listening, perceiving, and observing employee behavior closely during the rightsizing process, as we will discuss further in the next chapter.

Management Concerns

The rightsizing effort must be led by management. That is, all members of management must lead by example throughout the entire rightsizing process. One of the most often-heard complaints in an organization that was rightsized incorrectly is that, "They rightsized everybody except the executive level, where it was really needed."

To ensure that the rightsizing process is indeed management led, these attributes must be part of the rightsizing effort:

- Initial cuts must first be made at the level of vice president, associate administrator, or senior departmental director.
- No particular department or segment of the organization should be exempt from rightsizing, unless completely justifiable.
- If at all possible, an equal percentage of managers should be dismissed in proportion to an equal amount of employees.
- Managers should exhibit and communicate to their employees the sacrifices they are making as a result of the rightsizing. For example, managers can indicate the lack of available resources in their financial budget, a lack of personnel, or other detrimental conditions caused by the rightsizing, so employees understand that there is no difference between the effect of rightsizing on managers and employees.
- Managers should act appropriately emotional, though never denigrating the organization during the rightsizing process. That is, it is all right for managers to "act human" through the rightsizing process, so employees know that they are not alone in terms of their disgust, disenchantment, and distaste for the rightsizing effort.

Managers should make a conscious effort to support their "superstar" and "steady" employees throughout the rightsizing process. This extra effort in communication, empathy, and listening, as we have discussed, goes a long way to prevent a chasm between employees and management during rightsizing.

Other Considerations

The rightsizing effort must be effective and efficient, and it must balance quality with speedy, timely, and appropriate action. This includes:

- an immediate freeze on hiring new employees until all existing employees are rightsized, transferred, or placed in other positions;
- clear, concise, and objective communication;
- using early retirements, transfer to part-time status, and other permanent job shifts that can help alleviate the effect of rightsizing;
- using the entire volunteer corps of the hospital to help alleviate job stress, and using those capable volunteers appropriately;
- the participation of physicians and other extrinsic stakeholders in the entire process, to include the overall understanding of operating with shrinking resources in times of change and crisis;
- the increase of formal communication throughout the organization, including additional CEO "town meetings" and other forums that will provide an open dialogue, between employees and managers;
- completing entire rightsizing process within two months;
- completing the entire reconstruction process within six months; and
- completing the entire renewal process within four to six months.

By ensuring that the reorganization is effective and efficient, the institution demonstrates that it is acting with urgency, fortitude, and speed in the best interests of the customer/patient. This will be recognized by all staff members who are truly motivated and committed to the organization.

Gaining Future Ground

The entire reorganization effort must be "ground-gaining" or progressive—that is, it should be centered on gaining more ground in terms of resources, patients, service provision, and the other measurable gains that are reflected in the performance of a strong healthcare organization. The resources that should be realized by a progressive organization include:

- better, more skilled personnel;
- increased technical capabilities;
- increased efficiency and effectiveness of care;
- increased patient utilization;

- saving of time and energy in care delivery processes;
- a more cohesive use of personnel;
- a more consistent use of technology;
- improved care; and
- improved productivity.

Progress along these lines can be measured in two ways. First, a timeline can be drawn representing the entire year of the reorganization process. At three-month intervals, improvements—as noted in the list above—can be cited. For example, if a measurable gain has been achieved in a certain patient care area, it should be charted at three-month intervals and directly linked to the reorganization effort.

A second way to indicate how these important goals are being achieved is the use/comparison contrast. This would simply take a "before/after" dimension and indicate which gains have been achieved by the reorganization.

Finally, there are some mutual benefits that should be cited as part of the reorganization effort, which should be established as objectives at the beginning. The apparent benefits of the entire reorganization effort should include opportunities that:

- save time;
- save money;
- increase revenue;
- eliminate waste of time;
- waste of energy;
- eliminate a "hassle";
- eliminate the "headaches" of the administration process;
- improve quality;
- increase productivity;
- enhance communication;
- are good for the healthcare institution's future;
- will produce information that reveals something "new and different";
- will make the organization more user-friendly for customer/patients;
- decrease staff's boredom;
- help the organization meet a jurisdictional, organizational, or regional mandate, which in turn will allow for progressive healthcare delivery;
- increase the effectiveness of the healthcare delivery process;
- decrease negative performance;
- increase positive performance;

- increase the perception among the stakeholder community that the organization is a decent, ethical healthcare provider;
- demonstrate that the organization possesses organizational fortitude. In fact, undertaking the rightsizing process should demonstrate that the institution is indeed committed to becoming a "leaner and greener" healthcare provider;
- increase the integrity of the organization by eliminating positions that are not totally necessary;
- increase the organization's overall knowledge base and level of technical expertise;
- further enhance organizational stability;
- improve workplace safety;
- improve security;
- negate an apparent problem;
- address a perceived problem or threat;
- remedy an organizational weakness;
- counter an organizational threat;
- take the opportunity to redirect the organization to a progressive, future-focused path;
- build on an established organizational strength;
- build a positive public relations perception;
- correct an underlying, latent, potential problem;
- empower organizational members so they can act as independent contributors and interdependent colleagues in a new, progressive healthcare organization;
- aid in the further development of all employees, who will grow nominally through the rightsizing processes and exponentially during the reconstruction and renewal process;
- demonstrate community commitment by making the necessary changes; and
- prove that the organization is ready, willing, and able to make necessary change in the interest of the majority of its employees, as well as the customer/patient.

As mentioned at the beginning of this chapter, forming a strategic plan for reorganization is the most important part of the process, and the healthcare leader must take into account the many dimensions discussed this far. Once the decision to reconstruct—and downsize—has been reached and the strategic plan formulated, the outplacement process must be considered, and the ways to do this effectively will be analyzed in the next section.

Planning the Outplacement Process

Outplacement services provide dismissed employees the opportunity to take inventory of their specific skills and career desires, prepare a job search strategy, and take the initial steps to securing new employment. It is the opinion of the author and many leading healthcare consultants that no rightsizing should take place without at least a nominal outplacement effort. Outplacement services indicate a sense of organizational decency and integrity to the displaced employee, and they serve a tremendous public relations value to the surrounding community. In this section, we will explore the role of the organization as well as the manager in outplacement, contracted provider requirements, internal provider requirements, and who should receive outplacement services.

An outplacement plan should be formed practically, include a definite timeline, and incorporate the participation of several managers. It should also be administered by the organization's human resources department. The senior executive should have the final approval of the outplacement plan. The relative cost of outplacement services should be taken into consideration with the proportionate amount of community goodwill and positive impact on employee morale resulting from the outplacement effort. In essence, community members as well as retained employees will "feel better" about the rightsizing effort if a concerted effort was extended by the organization to help find new jobs for those displaced by the rightsizing process.

The organization's role in outplacement is manifold, but most importantly, it should select the outplacement firm quickly. Many consulting firms provide outplacement services, and it is sometimes difficult for healthcare executives, who have had little experience in outplacement firm selection, to make a clear determination on who would best provide services to their organization. Therefore, when selecting an outplacement firm, the organization should take these factors into account:

1. **Interview presentation**. All proposed outplacement contractors should visit the healthcare organization for an interview presentation. In this presentation, they should present a set of their credentials, a list of their experience with various clients—particularly those in healthcare—and a specific plan for the outplacement services for that healthcare facility.

2. **Established reputation**. Many healthcare consulting firms have established reputations in healthcare management, but not in outplacement. Conversely, many outplacement firms have established reputations in outplacement, but not in healthcare. Both types of firms, however, must have a deep knowledge of the healthcare industry. Our profession

is unique, and finding a new position for a healthcare executive is very different than locating a position for an executive in another field.

3. **Healthcare-specific expertise.** As mentioned in the previous point, it is vital that the outplacement firm know the changing world of healthcare and can provide point-specific expertise in this area. This can be exhibited in the interview presentation by use of various firms, citation of references within healthcare, and an explanation of previous success with healthcare clientele.

4. **Experience in the geographical area.** This is essential to the success of the outplacement effort. Many sectors of the United States and Canada have specific, unique nuances that affect new employment. A national consulting firm, for example, might have regional offices in a particular area of the United States but very little expertise or developed contacts to help displaced healthcare employees find work in that area. This factor must be investigated closely by the selection team of the rightsizing organization.

5. **References and other "track record" substantiation.** It is perfectly appropriate for a healthcare executive and the selection team to ask a consulting firm to provide specific references. However, it is wise for the executive and selection team to ask first for permission to contact those references to ask specific questions.

6. **Communication and listening ability.** The outplacement firm's ability to communicate and listen during the interview is usually a microcosmic look at how these individuals conduct their consulting approach. If the individual consultant making the presentation appears to be genuinely interested in the welfare of the displaced employees, and is clear and concise in his or her communication, chances are that these characteristics will appear in the actual consulting outplacement effort.

7. **Adaptability.** A "one size fits all" approach to outplacement can be deadly. It is imperative, therefore, for the chief executive in the selection team to generate as many examples from the consultant on various approaches to outplacement that they have utilized with past clientele. Strong marks should be given for creativity, innovativeness, individual attention, and "taking the extra step" in providing healthcare outplacement services.

8. **Follow-up strategies.** The consultant should be candidly asked, "What do you do to follow up with the displaced candidates from the outplacement process three months after the process takes place?" This is a crucial question of outplacement quality. In many cases, a good outplacement consulting firm will be able to provide numerous examples of "staying close" with a candidate until new employment is found.

9. **Educational ability**. Perhaps the most overlooked attribute of an outplacement consulting firm is its ability to educate not only the displaced personnel about its job search efforts and other pertinent dimensions but also to keep management informed of outplacement progress and to educate retained employees on the progress of the outplacement effort. This can be a very useful supplement to the organization's effort in not only rightsizing but in subsequent reconstruction and renewal.

After selecting the outplacement consulting firm, it is the responsibility of the organization's hierarchy to educate managers and other stakeholders on the contracting of the outplacement firm. It is essential that all managers within the healthcare organization explain to their employees that an outplacement service has been contracted for the displaced employees at the expense of the organization. The organization should also appropriately publicize the severance package given to displaced employees. This should be done in the notification letter (discussed in Chapter 3) to both the dismissed and retained employees. With appropriate confidentiality, the organization must give retained employees the message that their displaced colleagues are not only receiving a fair, equitable severance package, but their benefits are being continued.

The organization's responsibility in the outplacement process extends to assuring all dismissed employees that their outplacement process will be monitored consistently and that the outplacement firm will generate results. That is, employees must be promised that neither organization nor the outplacement firm will leave the displaced employees "high and dry" in a disinterested, noncommittal fashion. From a public relations standpoint, it is important that the organization promote results of the outplacement effort openly and fully evaluate the outcomes of the process. This should not only be part of the initial plan but should be done throughout the rightsizing process.

Many times, the author is asked, "Who should receive outplacement services?" Ideally, *anyone* who is displaced from the organization should, including executives and "high profile" individuals, technical staff, and high supply/low demand technical categories of personnel, such as dietary or housekeeping staff. However, the outplacement effort should also extend to recent hires—those who have been displaced from the organization after an unusually short tenure through no fault of their own. Long-term employees should also receive outplacement services, if for no other reason than out of respect for their long years of service. Certainly, good performers—that is, "superstar" and "steady" performers—should receive every extent of outplacement services. Finally, homogeneous groups—for example, a group of psychiatric nurses—should not only avail themselves of outplacement services but can be provided such services as a group.

Some healthcare executives believe that "nonplayers" should not receive outplacement services. This is a particularly questionable legal position—and certainly ethically speculative. By excluding "nonplayers" from the outplacement effort, the executive group at a healthcare organization is, put bluntly, asking for trouble. Obviously, if "nonplayers" are excluded from the outplacement process, they have a perfect opportunity to vilify the organization.

During the outplacement process, the manager must understand the scope and delivery of the outplacement firm's services. Furthermore, in certain cases, the manager can be the catalyst by introducing the outplacement services to the displaced employees. It is also helpful for the manager to provide the outplacement firm with appropriate insight into assisting the consultant provide specific outplacement care to that individual.

Furthermore, managers can provide references for the outplaced employee. They can additionally provide contacts and potential avenues of new employment, as well as assist in skills assessment and other pertinent activities, such as the composition of a new résumé. The manager naturally can support the processes specifically requested, for example, by providing additional insight into a particular displaced individual, or by providing extra contacts for that individual if the manager is particularly adept at generating contacts within a specific technical field.

Some healthcare organizations do not use trained outplacement specialists to conduct the outplacement effort. For such assistance, rather, they have turned to human resources department professionals; trained line-managers; their educational department; or local resources, such as local employment agencies. This practice is perfectly appropriate in an organization that cannot afford an outplacement firm. Also, a smaller healthcare organization can perhaps more efficiently use the services of individuals other than trained professional outplacement consultants.

Regardless of who provides outplacement services, however, six abilities must be demonstrated by individuals rendering those services:

1. the ability to garner trust from both management and staff, as well as displaced employees and retained employees;
2. the ability to demonstrate clearly a sense of expertise in listening, communicating, and providing appropriate emotional support to displaced individuals;
3. the ability to "close the loop"—that is, moving the employees' focus from their previous employer to the need to find new work;

4. the ability to provide appropriate counseling to displaced employees;
5. the ability to establish contact with new employers and to communicate effectively with any agency that might assist displaced employees; and
6. the ability to work with managers to inform them of both general outplacement progress and specific details of a particular displaced employee.

Outplacement is not only a management necessity, it is also a strong public relations tool. Outplacement should be the final stage of preparation, as outplacement automatically leads to the rightsizing process.

"House Rules"—Part II

Throughout the entire reorganization, all managers in a healthcare organization should adopt twenty "house rules." Unlike the five "house rules" listed earlier in this chapter, these rules pertain to how leaders and managers interact with the staff:

1. Always remember that you are in the spotlight, and the great majority of your staff will take action based on what they see you do.
2. No problems should be suggested by any employee throughout the entire process without your asking him or her to suggest a solution.
3. The power of pronouns should always be understood by all managers, to include the use of "we" as opposed to "us" and "them."
4. You must communicate as soon as possible and as much as possible in all situations.
5. Encouragement should be given to all "superstars" and "steady" employees, and "nonplayers" should be confronted as they try to derail the process.
6. Suggestions should be elicited from the staff and used if they are useful, progressive, realistic, practical, and viable.
7. Customer service in general, and patient care in particular, must not be compromised at any time throughout the process.
8. The patient community, replete with needs for new services and new types of care, should be the focal point of the reorganization of the facility.
9. Trust should be an absolute, and given to all "steady" and "superstar" employees and managers.

10. Any "wins" should be celebrated quickly, clearly, and comprehensively.
11. Progress should be publicized at every conceivable opportunity.
12. We must communicate what we are doing, and more importantly *why* we are doing it at every conceivable opportunity.
13. Staff should be constantly educated on change dynamics.
14. Staff should educate each other on change dynamics.
15. Leaders should make decisions quickly and resolutely.
16. Leaders should constantly listen, observe, and perceive communication.
17. If there is a bias when making subjective decisions, the bias should be to the patient.
18. Decency, fortitude, integrity, and industry should be driving values.
19. Focus on the future, not the past.
20. Everyone in the organization is accountable and is a leader in the process.

How most of these "house rules" are to be used will be discussed later. Using them in the healthcare leader's reorganization efforts will yield immediate positive benefits.

RIGHTSIZING

Past the clichés, rightsizing is a compelling force on industry in general, and specifically within the healthcare profession. Reengineering organizational action is meaningless with the wrong "mix" of staff and managerial talent. This chapter specifically reviews the best way—in terms of both ethics and economics—to rightsize the healthcare organization that facilitates short-term maximum performance and long-term promise. The rightsizing process must be managed artfully, intelligently, and with an ultimate focus on creating an organization prepared for the necessary reconstruction and renewal, which will ultimately help benefit the customer/patient.

Until recent times, the word "rightsizing" was anathema to most healthcare professionals and was, in fact, a "dirty word." There are many reasons for this, and perhaps the easiest explanation is that most healthcare professionals believed that rightsizing took place in many other industries but never within the healthcare service sector. Of course, times have changed drastically in the past several years, as we have discussed in previous chapters. Currently, most healthcare professionals recognize not only that rightsizing is indeed a fact of life, but is an unfortunate reality, mandatory to the survival of a healthcare organization. If properly managed, the rightsizing process can lay the foundation for a new, vibrant organization. If poorly managed, it can become perhaps the singularly most dangerous threat to organizational survival and a major cause for employee turnover and destruction of organizational morale; at its worst, rightsizing can cause the demise of the heretofore successful healthcare organization.

In this chapter, we will review the essential ethics of the rightsizing process, which should be displayed by all managers and executives. We will then analyze the communication process during rightsizing, as well as the actual process of enacting a reduction in force. Finally, we will conclude by discussing the "do's and don'ts" of rightsizing for managers and supervisors throughout the organization. Incorporating all of these approaches into the rightsizing effort will dramatically increase the likelihood that the outplacement will be successful, will create the least amount of damage, and will ultimately ensure the future success of the organization.

In our opening chapter, we discussed the stewardship responsibilities of a healthcare leader during the process of rightsizing, reconstruction, and renewal. The senior executive must adhere to a set of value-driven actions during *any* process of change, especially when the personal lives of employees will be drastically affected. In this section, we will revisit some of those stewardship responsibilities and discuss the essential ethics of decency, compassion, fortitude, introspection, and commitment—ethics that must be embraced by both the organization and its management when rightsizing.

The Ethic of Decency

Decency is the first defining ethic. Perhaps the most pragmatic definition of decency is the ability to act ethically in any given situation. Most healthcare employees will describe an executive as lacking decency if action is taken on the part of the organization in general—or the executive in particular—that disregards the personal life of a given employee. A specific example of this during the rightsizing process would be the perceived poor treatment of an individual whose job is eliminated as viewed by individuals in the organization who retain their job. While those individuals who are still employed are grateful that they still have a job, they will ultimately be fearful, mistrustful, and resentful toward the organization that seemingly eliminated their fellow worker's position without any sincere regard for his or her personal or professional life and well-being.

Accordingly, the organization must ensure that it rightsizes as "decently" as possible. As we discussed in the previous chapter, the planning process must be conducted intelligently, and a certain amount of common sense must be used when determining which jobs will be eliminated and which positions will be kept. If the plans for the new organization have been established before conducting a strong communication analysis, such as the change readiness index, the organization can demonstrate a sense of decency simply by acknowledging the importance of two-way communication throughout the entire process. In addition to surveys, the change readiness index, and other instruments, honest discussions with employees regarding their suggestions and input in how the organization might best redirect its efforts can be seen as a decent approach to a seemingly negative situation.

Perhaps the most decent way an organization can rightsize, however, is to do it quickly, accurately, and forthrightly. Time and speed are vital during a rightsizing process. Consider the example of a healthcare organization that knew for at least a year that a rightsizing action was needed. The administrator of the hospital believed that the "decent thing to do" would be to wait until the end of the year to see if the hospital's financial results miraculously "turned around," thus enabling the hospital to retain all of its existing employees. Naturally, with the healthcare industry then beginning to see the advent of managed care, and precarious new fiscal conditions, the economic picture did not improve by the end of the year; in fact, the financial results of the hospital were significantly worse than anticipated.

As a result, the prevailing conditions at the hospital by the end of the year were anything but decent. Three trends occurred that reinforce the importance of making the cut as quickly as possible. First, employees who were well-skilled, motivated and competent—and under the threat of a possible rightsizing throughout the course of the year—sought employment elsewhere and left the hospital for better positions. Second, the "nonplayers" were able to spread rumors and conjecture that increased the fear and poor morale among hospital employees. Third, most of the employees recognized from the reduction in census and empty beds throughout the facility that the hospital was indeed in financial trouble. Therefore, they knew that a cut was coming. The fact that the administrator failed to make the cut—that is, enact a rightsizing effort— indicated to the employees that in addition to being unaware, indecisive, and incompetent, the administrator did not care about their worklife, or else a cut would have been made quickly. The employees perceived that that would have been the "decent" thing to do. As one employee told the author during the outplacement process, "They had to know for the entire year that we had to do this. You think they would have done it quickly, and helped us to get jobs, rather than waiting to the end of the year, when they were just holding out for their bonus."

Of course, the reality in this case was different than the perceptions of this particular employee, but always remember that when rightsizing, **perception is *more* important than reality**. It is easy to understand, additionally, that the negative perceptions held by the employees can transcend themselves into the community as well.

Accuracy

Second, the rightsizing process must be accurate; the number of people and positions to be eliminated must be precise. Healthcare executives must strive to make certain that the cut is deep enough, but not so deep that some individuals will have to be hired back, either at the end of the rightsizing process or soon after. If individuals must be hired back because executive management made too deep a cut, the organization can be seen as being flatly incompetent and incapable of managing a healthcare institution during changing times.

Even worse, especially from the employees' point of view, is not making a deep enough cut in positions and personnel. Fundamentally, many healthcare organizations underestimate the number of positions or individuals that must be eliminated, and, as a result, they find that within months, another rightsizing must take place. This is detrimental for obvious reasons, but the worst problem is forcing the employees to go through a second rightsizing occurring immediately after the initial, emotionally charged one. Additionally, the organization can then be accused—rightfully so—by staff members as being incompetent.

Particular positions and departments must be downsized or eliminated accurately. In considering accuracy as part of the rightsizing process, healthcare executives must hold foremost in their thoughts that the prevailing perception among employees is "It might be me." Furthermore, after the rightsizing process takes place, the employees might think, having been fortunate enough still to have their job that "It might be me *next time*." If accuracy is considered an essential part of the rightsizing process, the employees' fears can at least be abated, if not eliminated, by witnessing first-hand a fair, accurate rightsizing. In summary, accuracy reflects effective action, which reflects thoughtfulness, which in turn demonstrates that the organization acted in a decent manner.

Forthrightness

An organization must act in a forthright manner during the critical time of rightsizing. Essentially, healthcare professionals need information along these four lines to feel that the organization has communicated with them honestly during the rightsizing effort:

1. when the rightsizing will take place;
2. who will be affected;

3. whether rightsizing will be a "one-shot deal" or additional rightsizing will be needed in the near future; and

. 4. what life will be like in the organization after rightsizing.

Ideally, as noted in the last chapter, the organization will explain the need for change and, specifically, the need for rightsizing. However, it is essential that all communication about rightsizing—from both the corporate level as well as the departmental and individual level—reiterate *why* rightsizing must take place. A review of some of the factors cited in Chapter 1 regarding the need for rightsizing could be used, and specific examples of conditions within the hospital—such as low census, decrease in inpatient utilization, or the needed elimination of certain services—can also be used in management-staff discussions.

However, every available means of communication should be used to express the need, the timing, and the specific conduct of the rightsizing action. As indicated in Figure 3.1, a short, specific letter should be sent to

---

Figure 3.1   Sample All-Staff Notification Letter

From: Kim Nicholas, CEO

To: All Staff

Subj: Upcoming Organizational Action

As many of you realize, the changing healthcare environment and our need to meet the needs of our service community dictate that certain changes must take place to ensure the viability and progress of our organization. Unfortunately, often these needs mandate unpleasant and unfortunate action.

During the next two months, our institution will undergo a reduction in force that will affect several members of our organization. Individuals whose job positions are affected by this action are receiving notification of their position elimination at this time. Within the next few days, all members of the organization will receive additional information regarding our new direction and focus.

I assure all staff that our actions will be conducted with a maximum of confidentiality, decency, and integrity. Outplacement services will be provided to all impacted individuals, and your managers—as well as those of us in the executive offices—stand ready to answer all questions and resolve any concerns you might have.

I look forward to your support as our organization perserveres through this difficult time, which will lead to a renewal of our commitment to our organization and community.

Sincerely,

Kim Nicholas
CEO

all staff citing the need for rightsizing and expressing a general timeline on when the actions will take place. This will dispel rumors that might be generated by the "nonplayers" and will also allow the majority of staff to understand that, because of the timeline, their stress and concern about rightsizing will be short-lived.

As soon as an organization recognizes that rightsizing must take place, and after a plan is established for the rightsizing and reconstruction process, communication should be generated, as reflected in Figure 3.1, within two months of the actual rightsizing. This lets employees know that significant action will occur within sixty days of the memo and thus sets specific, definite parameters to the rightsizing action, eliminating some anxiety among the workforce. While such means of communication as newsletters, closed-circuit broadcasts, town hall meetings, and other methods can be used to supplement the rightsizing letter, the letter itself, generated by the chief executive officer, should come first.

Subsequent to the general letter, a specific letter must be sent by the appropriate executive to the individuals being rightsized. This letter, illustrated in Figure 3.2, is perhaps the most honest, open communication device available to a manager in a rightsizing effort. It lends clarity to the process, lends its empathy to the affected employee, and pledges organizational support for the employee's individual redirection. The letter is obviously a confidential document and should be delivered in person whenever possible. When the letter is delivered, each manager must express appropriate personal sentiments to the employee and reiterate his or her own pledge of commitment to the employee in finding a new job. This again underscores organizational decency, as well as the next critical component of value-driven rightsizing, compassion.

The Ethic of Compassion

Fundamentally, "compassion" represents the feeling of a "common passion" or a "common unity" toward a specific objective among a community. In healthcare, a humanistic trust exists between the patient and the healthcare organization. Individuals within a healthcare organization have a common passion for success, which is measured by the satisfaction expressed by a patient upon receiving excellent healthcare.

Compassion extends itself similarly to the rightsizing process. In essence, there is no way to put a "happy face" on the visage of rightsizing. It is a painful process, emotionally charged and distasteful in many elements. However, the amount of compassion expressed by an organization in general—and by each manager specifically—can help to redefine the

---

Figure 3.2   Sample Individual Notification Letter

From: Kim Nicholas, CEO

To: Frank McGivney

Dear Frank:

   As you realize, our facility has recently experienced a loss of revenue and a dramatic shift in our operational resources and performance. As a result, a number of positions will be eliminated. Unfortunately, this reorganization includes the elimination of your positon, effective [one month from letter date].

   Our healthcare organization recognizes its commitment to support you during this difficult period. As a result, we have contracted outplacement services to assist you in finding new employment, constructed an extension of our benefit plan, and will generate a substantial severance payment to you immediately. Your manager, Deke Rivers, will give you the details of these arrangements immediately.

   Subsequent to your discussion with Deke, please contact our human resources department if you require additional assistance.

   We have valued your service to our organization and will do everything possible to assist you in continuing your career in healthcare.

Sincerely,

Kim Nicholas
CEO

---

quality of an organization in a humanistic, progressive manner. We will describe here the rightsizing process from when the letter detailing the rightsizing is sent to all employees to when the manager brings a sense of closure to each affected employee.

In the last section, we advised presenting a letter to each individual whose position will be eliminated. As illustrated in Figure 3.2, the letter is objective, direct, and appropriately empathetic. Writing such a letter, however, is easy. The difficult part of rightsizing is when emotionalism and interpersonal conflict arise as they always do when the letter is received. It then becomes the responsibility of the individual manager delivering the letter to schedule an exclusive, individual meeting with the employee. Ideally, the meeting should be scheduled close to the end of the day, so the employee can return home immediately afterward. This way, the employee will be guaranteed that his or her reactions will not be viewed by fellow colleagues. Further, detrimental employees will not be able to "vent" their emotions adversely in full view of their fellow employees.

Reactions to Rightsizing

Following the delivery of the notification letter, there are nine reactions employees can be expected to exhibit. We will discuss all of them and list specific strategies to manage the reaction, balancing compassion with the best interest of the employee and the organization.

Anger

The first apparent reaction will be *anger*, which usually occurs when the employee has no idea at all that he or she might be among the rightsized. On the other hand, the employee might very well have anticipated this and will use this opportunity to castigate the manager, negatively vent feelings about the organization or colleagues, or simply release any emotions he or she has been harboring about the rightsizing.

Whatever the cause, it is usually good practice for the manager simply to allow the affected employee the opportunity to vent. One can do this passively, by simply listening to the employee and responding nonverbally—such as with a nod of the head at appropriate times. In no case should the manager confront the employee, or make any statements that might elicit further anger. For example, some managers have made the mistake of saying, "If you would have performed at a higher level on your performance evaluation last year, perhaps we wouldn't have to have this discussion right now." This obviously does nothing to help the situation. Additionally, the manager should not make promises to the employee that cannot be fulfilled, such as suggesting that the employee might be rehired at a later date. This is not only foolhardy, but it could also become potentially litigious as the employee could use this as a *de facto* promise of reemployment.

If, during the conversation, the anger swells to an unusual level, it might be useful for the manager to get assistance from a senior manager or a member of the human resources staff. In fact, if the manager anticipates that the individual employee, based on previous examples of his or her work personality, might have an extraordinarily hostile reaction to the news, the manager might commence the meeting with a third party, such as a human resources professional or a senior manager, already present.

The final rule for dealing with the angry employee is to remember that when an individual begins to repeat statements, it is time to look for a conclusion to the discussion. That is, if the employee makes the same statement or charge—such as, "I don't think this is fair"— the manager might say, "We have endeavored to be fair with all of the employees affected. I'm sorry you do not agree with that assessment, but our discussing it further will not bring about any different resolution."

Additionally, at that point, the manager might suggest that the employee return home and consider the "total picture" of the rightsizing action; the manager should also reiterate that there will be no reconsideration of the rightsizing action.

Victimization

The second reaction among rightsized individuals is typically that of *victimization*, where the rightsized employee feels as though he or she has been unfairly singled out for rightsizing. This is a highly personal reaction, and one that is difficult for a manager to resolve. The employee who feels unfairly rightsized, and is thus a "victim," believes that he or she was dismissed because of their personality, ethnocentric background, or other nonwork-related feature. Of course, in an ethical organization this is *never* the case. However, allowing the perception that an individual was dismissed because of a personal characteristic can be extremely harmful, and in extreme cases, potentially litigious.

It is therefore essential for the manager to explain several facts to the employee to counter the perception of victimization. First, the manager must state that the employee will no longer be employed by the organization due to a host of business considerations, any one of an assortment of organizational mandates, or the likely possibility that his or her position will not be needed in the future. Fundamentally, the position analysis matrix of Chapter 2—relating to performance, potential, and progressive promise—must be explained completely and specifically to the individual's position.

Second, the manager can explain that the individual claiming victimization is not the only member of the organization who is being rightsized, which is a particularly convincing argument when other individuals in the same position have been dismissed.

Finally, when the affected employee claims that he or she was singled out for rightsizing, the manager should be able to cite another individual—without using specific names—eliminated from the organization who perhaps was employed for a longer period of time, a shorter period of time, in a higher-paying position, in a lower-paying position—or any other comparison that will refute the basic premise of the employee's perceived victimization.

It is essential, though, that the manager refrain from engaging in a "mind game" with the employee. Rather, the manager should just follow the script of the notification letter, not engage in hyperbole or emotionally charged discourse, and simply let the employee vent before closing the meeting.

Passivity

The third reaction on the part of an individual affected by a rightsizing is relatively easy to handle—the *passive* individual. Usually, this individual will read the notification letter and comment that he or she "expected it." These employees will have very little to say in the course of the discussion and may act relieved when receiving the letter. In this case, the manager can simply reiterate his or her commitment to help secure a new job if at all possible, to answer any questions through the transition process as required, and to volunteer any specific resources available to assist the affected employee.

When dealing with the passive employee, the manager must be observant for a delayed reaction: While the individual might initially be relieved that the rightsizing has finally occurred, after some thought and introspection he or she might act nefariously and vilify the organization. When this occurs, the manager should confront those employees directly and offer to expedite their outplacement to hasten their departure from the organization. In fact, the healthcare organization should do so whenever possible.

Shock

Some individuals clearly do not look at their organization's big picture—or they truly believe that certain organizational dimensions will never affect their jobs. In these cases, some individuals will be in complete *shock* when confronted with a notification letter. In this case, it is advantageous for the manager not to pursue a specific conversation with the individual but rather express interest in meeting with the employee a few days after he or she has the opportunity to think about the dismissal. In doing so, the manager is still fulfilling his or her responsibility to the employee but is allowing the employee the opportunity to respond to it individually and at the highest possible level of comfort.

Resentfulness

The fifth reaction is that of *resentfulness* on the part of the employee, which can almost appear to be vitriolic. As opposed to being merely angry, the resentful employee usually focuses anger on a specific entity, such as the manager, the organization, or the lack of performance on the part of a colleague. That is, the employee immediately blames someone else for his or her dismissal. On some occasions, these individuals can become violent, or at least verbally threatening to the organization, the manager, or a peer.

There is only one way to deal with resentful individuals: Immediately give them their final paycheck, a notification of the extension of their benefits, and any other components of the outplacement package, and make their dismissal effective at once. Under no circumstances should these individuals be allowed to remain and display their special breed of violence, malice, or other aberrant behavior. These individuals are not entitled to anything from the organization except for their requisite pay and extension of benefits.

Fear

The sixth reaction is that of *fear*. Upon receiving news that they are indeed part of the "rightsized population," certain individuals instantaneously become scared, usually because of the lack of future employment, along with all of the personal and family travails that situation entails. With these individuals, it is essential that the manager underscore the organization's commitment to provide outplacement services, as well as the manager's personal commitment to help them find a new job. Depending on the individual's past performance level, the manager should extend as much assistance as possible helping him or her in securing new employment. An additional step might be for the manager to facilitate an immediate discussion between the affected "scared" individuals and the human resources department or the outplacement agency. Most quality outplacement firms will work with managers directly and extend special consideration and more efficient action to those who might be more emotionally distraught over the loss of a job than their dismissed colleagues. In short, every consideration should be given to the individual who is profoundly affected by the rightsizing and has demonstrated adequate performance and allegiance to the organization.

Vengeance

The seventh reaction can best be depicted as an individual who becomes *vengeful* when receiving the news of downsizing. These individuals usually want to—to use common parlance—"get even with somebody" whom they believe is part of the process. They usually feel that "somebody" to be a boss, a colleague, or a particular employee who led to their undoing. This is largely speculative on their part, but the reality is that they sincerely believe that one individual was responsible for their loss of employment. This can become a dangerous situation with violent ramifications if not managed correctly.

The manager should do everything conceivable to convince these vengeful employees that no particular individual was responsible for their elimination from the organization. Furthermore, if the individual has accused a particular party as being responsible for his or her dismissal, the manager should use the human resources department or senior management to make certain that the individual cited by the vengeful employee is aware of those negative feelings. In some cases, security might be involved or perhaps a local public safety officer might be notified, but in all cases, it is absolutely imperative to make certain that the employee knows that negative repercussions of any kind will not be tolerated. Again, it is good managerial practice for the vengeful individuals to be immediately dismissed from the organization, after being given their final paycheck and extension of benefits. This immediately precludes any opportunity for them to act vengefully toward any remaining member of the organization.

Embarrassment

The eighth reaction is that of *embarrassment*. Some individuals will experience for the first time a sense of failure in their healthcare careers when they learn that they are among the rightsized. As we have seen throughout this section, even using the euphemism "the rightsized" carries a certain stigma such as "the damned." There is no way to evade this perception. Accordingly, individuals who throughout their career have worked hard and contributed positively to the organization now find themselves being outplaced through no fault of their own. Embarrassment would be a logical reaction.

The best response for a manager is simply to tell the employee the facts: First, our organization is rightsizing because of a confluence of external factors, not because of your individual performance. Second, many individuals in the organization are seeing their positions eliminated because of these reasons, and you are not being singled out because of a failure on your part to perform at an adequate level. Third, there is no need to be embarrassed; many healthcare professionals across the country are being rightsized—almost every day—simply because of changes within the profession. Finally, with an efficient job search, a new position in healthcare—or perhaps even in another industry—should be available for a talented individual; with the assistance of the outplacement effort and the manager's personal support, perhaps such a position will be found sooner rather than later.

It is essential that the embarrassed individual be allowed to "save face" among his or her colleagues. Therefore, the delivery of the notification letter to an individual whom the manager presumes will feel embarrassed and dejected should be scheduled at the very end of the workday so that the individual can leave the facility without being observed by any colleagues. In short, the manager should do everything possible to preserve the dignity of the well-meaning, solid organizational player who feels embarrassment in the face of rightsizing.

Betrayal

Finally, almost every individual who is rightsized feels a certain amount of *betrayal*. This is logical, but unfortunately this feeling cannot be logically countered. In reality, something has betrayed the individuals who are being rightsized. It could be the healthcare profession, which changed more rapidly over the past ten years than the healthcare planners could have imagined. Or, it could be blamed on healthcare administrators, who in certain areas of the country did not possess enough respect for the changing needs or rising expections of their customer/patients. In any case, a sense of compassion must be extended to all individuals affected by a rightsizing, augmented by a pledge on the part of every manager and organizational member to assist in a smooth move to a new position.

The Ethic of Fortitude

Managers who participate in a rightsizing effort at a healthcare organization must embrace fortitude as part of their contribution. Fortitude basically refers to the ability to make tough calls in tough circumstances. If a healthcare manager prior to 1990 did not possess the characteristic of fortitude, they most certainly possess it by the time they read this book: The immense amount of change and negative conditions that have affected the healthcare profession over the past five years have tempered managers with the ability to react positively in bad situations.

"Do's and Don'ts" of Rightsizing

In this section, we will discuss managerial fortitude and review a set of practical "do's and don'ts" that a manager must embrace. These "do's and don'ts" were compiled by asking over 100 managers involved in a rightsizing process to list—based on their personal and professional experience—the best ways to handle a difficult situation.

Don't get overly emotional. When managers get emotional, staff members pay more attention to the "show" than the "substance," and will react accordingly, particularly in times of change when they look to a leader to demonstrate the proper response to a particular situation. For example, if a manager becomes fearful, employees will assume that the worst is about to happen. If a manager becomes angry with administration, employees—especially if they like and respect their manager—will sense that administration might be unfair throughout the rightsizing process. In another regard, if a manager becomes emotionally distraught about one individual being rightsized from the organization, the entire staff might advocate retaining that individual, despite the fact that in order for the rightsizing to be fair, the position must be eliminated.

Therefore, it is important for the manager to stay as objective as possible in all situations. Certainly a manager, as a human being, must and should respond emotionally in certain situations—but not to the extent that it creates an undesirable response with the staff. If the manager decides that something requested by the administration is unfair, it is his or her responsibility to take that up directly with the administration, and not to reflect his or her feelings to the staff. If managers become angry or distraught during the rightsizing process, it is essential that they take their emotions behind the closed doors of their office, not in a common area where it could be observed by staff. As we have discussed, fear is a very contagious emotion within a healthcare staff and does not need to be enhanced by the participation of a manager, or else the rightsizing process will become more charged than it already is.

Don't "overtalk" in any phase. This refers to the "overpromising" that takes place when managers try to compensate for the negativity of rightsizing with the promises of future benefits. For example, many times in a rightsizing effort a manager will state, "The rightsizing will make us stronger in the future." Ideally, this is true. However, if the manager says that the organization will "be greater than it ever has been before," or "This will allow us to make even more money" or any other specious promise, both the manager and the organization will lose credibility when these promises are not fulfilled.

This extends to an individual level. During rightsizing, a manager should not, for example, promise that one employee will now have the opportunity to undertake responsibilities he or she previously desired or will have the funds available to innovate a project he or she has been planning. A serious breach of trust will take place between the manager and the employee if the rightsizing does not immediately result in an immediate positive gain. Rather, it is incumbent upon the manager to speak realistically about the rightsizing effort and energize the staff toward focusing on immediate needs.

Don't take anything personally. When frightened, people will say or do anything. They may question the manager's integrity or castigate him or her personally. It is difficult for a manager not to take such insults personally, particularly if he or she is under stress, which will naturally occur during the rightsizing process. However, managers must keep in mind that their allegiance to the organization, their dedication to their profession, and most importantly, their intentions to take adequate care of the customer/patient as well as their staff are more important than the epithets of a rightsized former employee.

Most essentially, it is vital for managers to remember that they do not have to listen to an employee's personal attacks. When a rightsized employee becomes verbally abusive, the manager can simply say, "I don't get paid enough money to listen to these personal attacks. This conversation is now over." If necessary, the manager can immediately notify security to remove the individual from the premises. Therefore, it is best to prevent such verbal attacks before they take place. Additionally, every senior executive involved in a rightsizing organization should ensure that all managers know that they do not have to take undue verbal abuse from any employee under any circumstance. It is truly surprising how many managers believe that such insults are part of the job description for the modern healthcare manager. It simply is not, and such personal attacks have no redeemable, useful end.

Do listen, observe, and perceive. During the rightsizing process, all managers must listen to *what* each employee says. In times of fear and change, managers often do not get the complete picture of an employee's expression. Rather, they listen only to what they need to hear, or to those components of communication that have immediate urgency. First, the manager should strive to listen to the general context—and specifically, to the small details—of an employee's message about work performance, the rightsizing itself, or other critical dimensions during the two-month rightsizing process.

Second, it is vital for the manager to observe *how* the employee communicates. Without becoming an "amateur psychologist," the manager should logically observe employees' speech patterns, their nonverbal communication, and any other "clues" that might indicate the manner in which they are expressing themselves, which in turn might indicate to the manager the employees' emotions behind a specific situation.

Finally, the manager should understand *why* the employee is presenting a certain message. If the manager cannot immediately ascertain why an employee is saying something, he or she should bluntly ask, "Why are you saying that?" or "Why do you feel it necessary to tell me this?" Communication is certainly the key to success in a rightsizing effort, and managers should make every effort possible to ensure that they are collecting as much input from employees, past organizational surveys and other formal instruments. However, by simply listening to what an employee says, the manager might not capture the motive, intent, and sentiment behind the employee's participation. Therefore, the continuous listening, observation, and perception of employee discourse is essential throughout the rightsizing effort.

Do ask questions at any point in the process. Any time is a good time for a question in the rightsizing process. These questions can be addressed to managers and senior executives about the conduct of the rightsizing, or they can be asked by the manager to the employee about reactions, morale, and most importantly, suggestions for performance improvement. It is also notable that most successful healthcare organizations have doubled the number of management meetings during rightsizing efforts.

For example, if managers meet with executives once a month, during the rightsizing sequence they should meet twice a month. In cases where employees meet biweekly with managers, meetings should be conducted weekly. This brings about two positive outcomes. First, employees will see that the organization believes the rightsizing to be a unique event, during which employee communication will be particularly valued. Second, it provides managers with the opportunities to follow-up quickly on certain issues and exhibit a sense of continuity from one meeting to the other. Because things happen so fast during rightsizing, "doubling up" scheduled meetings provides an excellent opportunity to keep everyone—managers and staff alike–informed.

Logically, these meetings become an opportunity to ask questions. There are five types of questions that provide the best answers about the rightsizing process:

1. questions to get information;
2. questions to investigate particular feelings and sentiments;
3. questions to determine future plans;
4. questions relative to community and external reaction; and
5. questions leading to assessment of rightsizing efforts to date.

At no time should questions that lead to "second-guessing" be asked during the rightsizing process. Such questions as, "Did we really do a good job at this?" have no useful purpose until the entire rightsizing process is completed. During the effort itself, questions should be specifically asked about the continuous conduct of the rightsizing effort.

Don't say, "I understand." By saying, "I understand," the manager is giving any employee the opportunity to say, "No, you don't!" What the manager should say is, "I can appreciate how you feel." As simple as it sounds, this gives the employee the perception that the manager does not know everything but is trying hard to turn a negative situation into a positive one. This type of response also allows employees the opportunity to educate the manager further about the specific needs and concerns they are trying to manage as the rightsizing occurs. When the manager says, "I understand," it completely eradicates any opportunity for the employee to feel as though the manager is open-minded to his or her input, suggestions, or concerns.

Don't think that your facility is unique in having to rightsize. In fact, very few institutions in the United States will *not* have to rightsize. In the author's experience with over 100 healthcare facilities in the past three years, only two facilities have not had to rightsize. Both of these facilities are uniquely located in parts of the United States with populations or economies that are growing by leaps and bounds—one in Hawaii and the other on the Texas-Mexico border. All of the other facilities have had to rightsize—and all for the same reasons that have been discussed throughout this text.

A good approach for dealing with employees who think "it can't happen here" is to compile a list of leading regional healthcare organizations that have had to rightsize—along with a list of prominent companies in other industries that were forced to dismiss staff members. This lays the foundation for an effective comparison/contrast exercise, which can usually open with, "If you would have said ten years ago that _____ had to rightsize, no one would have believed you. As we all know, they have had to rightsize." By using this exercise, management can inform staff that rightsizing is part of the business scene and, unfortunately, endemic to every healthcare organization.

Do network with other facilities and contacts. The healthcare profession has a strong industrial community, replete with effective networking ties. As virtually every healthcare organization in the United States has experienced or will experience some sort of rightsizing, a natural opportunity exists for healthcare managers to network with each other. With this in mind, it is useful to contact an individual you might have met at a seminar or attended college with who works for a rightsizing institution. These ten commonalities should be considered when networking:

1. size of your institutions;
2. rural, suburban, or urban location;
3. teaching affiliation;
4. type of financial structure;
5. past history of the organization;
6. management structure of the organization;
7. type of patient;
8. merger or acquisition variance;
9. future potential of the organization; and
10. surrounding community dynamics.

If you and your networking contact have at least five of these ten dimensions in common, there is probably a wealth of information you could share with each other about the rightsizing process. Remember, there are no absolutes or prescribed rules when it comes to rightsizing. As a profession, we are learning our lessons jointly on rightsizing, so every day is an opportunity to learn more about this process, and moreover, gain essential information that might be helpful in making your organization stronger at the end of the rightsizing, reconstruction, and renewal process.

Do stick with established themes. During the rightsizing process, as is the case with all organizational efforts, there exist some central themes as indicated in Figure 3.3, that need to be reiterated. In examining these twelve themes, a manager can create a sense of resonance with all staff members relative to the rightsizing effort. If staff members hear these themes consistently, constantly, and candidly, they will begin to echo throughout the organization, and create a sense of credibility.

However, when managers become creative in the communication process—or act like a victim during the rightsizing—disastrous results can occur. One example occurred in the author's experience where a manager of a quality improvement department decided that none of the rightsizing plan's mandates applied to her section. By constantly countering the organization's message, as well as by creating fear and distrust among most members of her department, the manager alienated not only the majority of her staff but created a schism with the other units within this organization. Upon reflection, the administrator of the organization realized that this "CQI" department had done precious little to increase revenue in the past, and its patient satisfaction scores were

Figure 3.3   Twelve Management Themes During Rightsizing

1. Patient Focus vs. "Nonplayer" Focus
2. Commitment to Mission vs. "100 Percent Consensus"
3. What We *Need* to Do vs. What We'd *Like* to Do
4. Clear Communication vs. Complication of Rumors
5. Fact of Actions vs. Fiction of Conjecture
6. Moving to the Future vs. Dwelling on the Past
7. Solving Problems vs. Reiterating Problems
8. Proaction vs. Reaction
9. Celebrating the Wins vs. Pondering the Losses
10. Group Communication vs. Individual Complaints
11. Contribution vs. Procrastination
12. Value-Driven vs. Self-Centered Victimization

at their absolute lowest. Inadvertently, this administrator realized that she had been victimized by the manager's rebelliousness and antipathy throughout the past seven years, but these sentiments became crystallized during the rightsizing process. The lesson learned by this particular CEO was that all managers should stick to a centralized set of themes, such as those displayed, without exception. In doing so, no one in the organization is led to believe that he or she is more important than anyone else, and thus immune to rightsizing.

Do extend the human touch as appropriate and based on merit. Everyone within the organization will have an unique reaction to the rightsizing. In all cases, it is essential for the manager to monitor staff reaction, and as appropriate, extend a sense of compassion to affected employees. The best approach is for the manager to look for employee work behavior that is different than normal. For example, if a gregarious employee becomes withdrawn, or a participative employee becomes passive, chances are rightsizing has taken an underlying, subconscious hold on them. At this point, it is important for the manager to intervene, perhaps by taking the employee to the cafeteria for a cup of coffee and a frank discussion.

During this discussion, the manager should ask some or all of these five questions:

1. How is this rightsizing affecting you?
2. Is there anything I can do to make this rightsizing go a little bit more smoothly?
3. Are there any resources that we have that you can use to get through the rightsizing a little bit more efficiently?
4. Is there something about the rightsizing that is particularly bothering you?
5. What can we do to help you weather the rightsizing?

From a purely business standpoint, the human touch should be extended specifically to individuals who could be classified as either "superstar," hard-driving staff members or "steady," solid organizational players. The "nonplayers," who are contentious and negative, should not be allowed an extended amount of "air time" in departmental meetings. In fact, if they have not been rightsized, a distinct message should be sent to the "nonplayers" that they are fortunate that they are still employed. This message should be sent primarily by the departmental manager, and augmented by a strident performance review, as appropriate, at the end of the grading period.

This last point best summarizes the entire issue of fortitude in the rightsizing process. Recently, a young manager at a Louisiana hospital was questioned by the author about what he considered to be the most difficult management dilemma of his career. The manager confided that soon he would have to rightsize three of his employees. However, all three employees were negative performers and were individuals who probably should have been terminated prior to his ascension into management.

Despite all of this, the young manager was concerned about dismissing these three employees because of their families—certainly a prevailing sentiment among all healthcare managers during times of termination, particularly during rightsizing. The author gave the manager advice that incorporated the subject of families: Fundamentally, the families of the existing employees, the families of those employees who will still be employed after rightsizing, and most importantly, the families of those cared for by the institution are the prevailing consideration in any rightsizing. Rightsizing occurs to make sure that these families are afforded the best type of employment, if their family members are employees, and the best healthcare services, if their families are part of the community the organization serves. To this end, rightsizing—in an indirect but very real fashion—helps to ensure that these families will receive the organization's benefit for years to come.

The Ethic of Introspection

Introspection is the ability to think ethically, clearly, and comprehensively about the consequences and actions relative to rightsizing. A certain amount of introspection is required for the manager to complete the rightsizing cycle at both the individual departmental level and the executive level.

In this section we will review a series of actions the manager should take to reflect integrity on the part of the organization and introspection and credibility on the part of that particular manager.

To begin with, the manager must understand that once the notification letter is delivered to the downsized individuals—those individuals whose positions have been eliminated—the remainder of the staff can best be classified as the "survivors," who will fall into several different categories. Common to all of these categories, however, is a set of reactions that all survivors will demonstrate.

For example, the majority of survivors will feel affirmed by the rightsizing action. That is, they will feel confident in the organization, not only because the organization made "the tough call," but because that "tough call" did not eliminate their job. Therefore, they will feel suitably grateful to the organization, and their belief in their own worthiness to the organization will be affirmed. This is a natural reaction, and certainly one the manager should use to the organization's advantage. Without being redundant or self-serving, the manager should take the opportunity immediately to meet with all of the individuals in his or her department and stress that he or she now has a team that is "lean, professional, and ready to go." Furthermore, the manager should affirm that the rightsizing was done fairly and correctly, and gave him the opportunity to work with a team of professionals that will be best geared for the future. This must be punctuated by a statement that the rightsizing was unfortunate, and that the manager wishes nothing but the best for the individuals who are no longer with the organization.

Another typical reaction on the part of the survivors is one of relief. Once again, this is both an instantaneous and natural reaction, as individuals will immediately believe that "the worst is behind them" as the rightsizing concludes. While this might be true, the prevailing ethic of introspection must now be extended to every individual. That is, each individual should reflect on why the rightsizing occurred to begin with, and make a specific commitment to make certain that the conditions that mandated it do not reoccur. For example, a food service department that was rightsized because of a shift from inpatient services to outpatient services should examine closely how to provide meals and snacks for outpatients, as well as offering food services for inpatients. In summary, the feeling of relief should be enjoyed in the short term by the surviving staff; then, it should be replaced by a long-term commitment to introspectively examine all opportunities for improving services to prevent the need for future rightsizing.

Among the surviving staff the feeling of guilt can be pervasive: The surviving members of the organization may feel guilty that they have their jobs while other individuals have been rightsized. This can be particularly true in organizations that rightsized based on tenure, rather than performance. In these situations, individuals who were recently hired—but were hard workers—may have been "let go" in favor of individuals who have been at the organization for a considerable amount of time but who may not have performed at a particularly exceptional level. In most situations, it is natural for surviving staff members to feel remorseful that some of their colleagues are no longer employed by the organization.

The best strategy is for the manager to confront these situations candidly and directly. The manager should say, "I would think that most of the individuals who worked at this organization previously who are no longer here would like us to do our best to make sure that this organization will always be one that they are proud of." Implicit to this statement is a call for the remaining staff to continue to make the organization a prosperous one out of respect for their colleagues who have left the organization. It is important to note that people will now feel guilty about keeping their job for too long. The realities of life are such that a good job in healthcare with a sound future is now a privilege.

A more typical reaction is that of appreciation to the organization. If a rightsizing is done correctly, an assortment of factors will be apparent for which the average employee will be appreciative. Fundamentally, the employee will appreciate that the organization:

- made the rightsizing fairly and quickly;
- preserved their job;
- demonstrated the necessary ability to adapt to change;
- recognized the fact that it had to rightsize to preserve the jobs of the majority of the employees; and
- rightsized rather than closed down, merged, or anything else that might be perceived as being more negative than a rightsizing.

From this appreciation comes a spark of loyalty. Most survivors of a rightsizing are indeed more loyal to the organization than they were previously, particularly if their job was preserved.

There exists a prevailing notion in sociology and the political lexicon that is termed "corporate responsibility." In its worst extreme, corporate responsibility refers to the accountability of an organization to maintain jobs—as well as benefits—for *all* of its employees *all* of the time. This theory is created by political scientists, political figures, and certain sociologists who do not understand the peculiarities of accelerating technology and fiscal shifts.

A better definition of corporate responsibility in healthcare is an organization that seeks to provide stellar service to its constituent community in return for customer/patient allegiance and commitment. To that end, a sense of loyalty must exist among employees and can certainly be inspired subsequent to a downsizing.

The staff manager should discuss with his or her team the answers to these five questions:

1. How can we get better?
2. How can we reconstruct our department to be more efficient?
3. If you were administration, what moves would you make to make the organization even more effective?
4. If you were the manager of this department, what moves would you make to make us more effective?
5. What things are you going to start doing tomorrow to make *you* more effective?

Fear is a tremendous motivator. Even before the rightsizing is over—and despite the best possible efforts to ensure that another one will not occur—any organization will experience a certain amount of conjecture that another round of dismissals will take place. While assuring staff that this is not true, the manager should underscore that the rightsizing served a purpose in teaching that the only constant in healthcare is change. Therefore, in order to be proactive, and ultimately successful, each employee is accountable for introspectively examining his or her position and determining the best possible course for future action.

The remaining emotions among the survivors include surprise that their jobs were maintained, skepticism that no rightsizing will occur in the future, a sense of apprehension toward the future, or simply a state of euphoria that the rightsizing has been completed and most individuals can return to their jobs. These are all valid emotions, and should be used collectively to spark a sense of recommitment to new ideas, new approaches, and open input, which are all crucial for the reconstruction effort.

The Ethic of Commitment and Some Practical Solutions

The final ethic that should be considered when rightsizing is commitment. For our discussion, commitment is the value that facilitates closure of the rightsizing process. After the "storm" of rightsizing, it is essential that the manager employ several strategies to help redefine commitment to the organization and its future.

In order to make this discussion regarding commitment as "user-friendly" as possible, we will employ a "point/counterpoint" format. This will allow the reader to look at specific problems and their appropriate answers or strategies.

Problem: People raising problems relative to the process. Throughout the rightsizing process, some contentious individuals will spotlight problems.

Solution: No problems without a solution. A house rule should be established stating that "no one can raise a problem without at least suggesting a solution." The solutions to these problems must be useful, viable, progressive, and practical. This allows everyone to be a contributor and a leader in the rightsizing process, as opposed to merely a spectator. If an individual is well meaning and well motivated, he or she will probably have thought of a solution before raising the problem. Individuals who are contentious by nature, when asked to present a solution to a particular problem, will usually say, "I don't know." This, of course, is utterly useless. By asking them to present a solution, however, they are being instructed, directly or indirectly, that they are accountable for solutions. This will be particularly important in the "post-reduction" phase, which takes place immediately after the rightsizing and staff may feel they have to do more with less.

Problem: What is the perfect solution in rightsizing? Despite networking, researching, and asking questions at all times, it is difficult to come up with a definitive solution to rightsizing.

Solution: Recognize there is no perfect solution. Essentially, each organization is unique in terms of its personnel, management, and particular conditions. Therefore, there is no set solution that would work the same way for every organization, although there are some general rules and some lessons that help create positive action. A line manager or senior executive should never become frustrated or angry that their rightsizing efforts are not flawless. This would simply be humanly impossible, as rightsizing forces one to deal with negative opinions, new situations, and a variety of other conditions that contribute to the impossibility of a perfect solution. Managers should *trust their instinct at all times*. Fundamentally, if the manager has a "bad feeling" about a particular segment of rightsizing, he or she simply should not pursue it. Collaborating with colleagues and listening to the concerns of employees help to complete a progressive rightsizing process.

Problem: "They" are making us rightsize. The pronoun "they" is ubiquitous in work discussions, particularly when negative circumstances are involved. "They" are usually administration. Managers can find themselves in an untenable position by castigating "they," agreeing with "they," or trying to defend "they." At that point, the employees will see the manager as either being part of the problem, a co-conspirator in the rightsizing process, or as an unwitting ally to the "nonplayers" who do not recognize the need to rightsize.

Solution: Use the collective "we." "No one wins unless we all win"— perhaps the one true adage in healthcare management in the 1990s. The victory being sought by healthcare organizations is simply to stay in business and thrive as future demands for healthcare accelerate. Every member of the organization is accountable. As soon as rightsizing takes place, the manager should use the pronoun "we" in these variations:

- *We* need to rightsize.
- *We* recognize that if we do not change we will not survive.
- *We* understand that our patients expect more of us.
- *We* understand that revenues are shrinking.

- *We* understand that certain positions are not as vital to the organization as they once might have been.
- *We* understand that rightsizing is not easy.
- *We* understand that all healthcare organizations must rightsize.
- *We* understand that our organization is one in which integrity is important; therefore, rightsizing will be as honorable and as equitable as possible.

If the manager is committed to these principles at the beginning of the rightsizing effort, and consistently uses the pronoun "we," the employees understand once again that they are participants in this process and not merely victims or spectators.

Problem: Employee productivity and performance dissipates during the rightsizing process. Perhaps the most pernicious effect of rightsizing is the lack of performance during the rightsizing cycle. This is common, as most employees feel that there is no reason for them to accelerate efforts if the organization is going to rightsize—and perhaps let them go. This is understandable, as most people do not want to work hard on behalf of an organization that is going to eliminate their job.

Solution: Bring closure to the rightsizing process. One of the reasons it is essential for a rightsizing process to take only two months is that employees' productivity naturally tends to drop during the rightsizing process. Therefore, if the rightsizing takes a year or two, the process itself might doom the organization because of the lack of productivity and decreasing performance.

Accordingly, once the rightsizing has concluded, it is essential for every manager, team leader, supervisor, and executive in the healthcare organization to make certain that all members of the organization realize that rightsizing has been concluded. This can be done in a variety of methods, such as:

- publishing the successes of the outplacement effort;
- writing a letter from the chief executive of the institution to all staff;
- reestablishing performance goals;
- introducing a new performance evaluation system; and
- immediately implementing any of the reconstruction and renewal strategies that will be discussed later.

Closure on the rightsizing process must be finite, absolute, and without regret. Once the rightsizing process has taken place, and every effort has been made to express the ethics described throughout this chapter, the executive can rest assured that he or she has done everything within their professional powers to make the rightsizing a fair, value-driven process. At that point, it becomes the responsibility of each organizational member to move on to the reconstruction phase of the process, or decide that their professional needs might be better served at another institution.

Problem: People dwelling on the past. When rightsizing occurs in an organization that has not been affected by an appreciable amount of change, the repercussions of the rightsizing could appear daunting. In essence, many individuals among the staff will look to the past fondly and wish that they were still operating in an era where they believe "healthcare did not change that much and was concerned about people and not the bottom line, and we did not have to rightsize."

Solution: Focus on the future. Unfortunately for those individuals who dwell in the past, there will never be a return to the fondly remembered bygone days of healthcare. Competition will increase, change will become rampant, and technology and customer/patient expectations will escalate. All healthcare practitioners in a supervisory, managerial, or executive level must understand clearly that it is their responsibility to encourage all members of their staff not only to focus on the future but to define programs, solutions, and approaches to meet tomorrow's demands. This sometimes involves the education of board members to healthcare change, publication of a comprehensive five-year organizational plan, and, of course, implementation of an immediate reconstruction and renewal plan.

Problem: The staff does not like the way the rightsizing occurred. No one, at least in the experience of the author or any of the experts that were consulted when writing this book, can remember an organization in which the overwhelming majority of staff and managers "liked" a rightsizing action. Nobody likes to see friends dismissed or positions reduced, and no one enjoys working with individuals who are scared, frustrated, and apprehensive about the future.

Solution: I can respect the way the organization conducted the rightsizing. This is the other side of the coin. Many healthcare organizations have rightsized successfully because the staff felt that it was conducted fairly and was necessary for the organization to succeed. In organizations where the rightsizing was considered fair, equitable, and effective, the following guidelines were followed throughout the process:

1. Never apologize for the need to rightsize after you already explained the *why* behind the rightsizing.
2. Emphasize that rightsizing is necessary to meet the needs of the customer/patient, which is the preeminent reason for the existence of a healthcare organization.
3. Be human, be respectful, and be a source of compassion at all times.

4. Encourage all members of the organization to act as accountable adults and professionals in the process.
5. Encourage your "superstars" to lead the way through the rightsizing.
6. Assist your "steady" employees with their work demands, emotional upheaval, or other changes.
7. Do not let the contentious "nonplayers" dominate the "air time" in meetings or other communication forums.
8. Do not revisit closed issues in the rightsizing—once something is done, move on to the next step.
9. Do not worry about overcommunicating—there is no such thing.
10. Follow your rightsizing schedule.
11. Always remember to extend the prevailing ethics of decency, compassion, commitment, introspection, and fortitude.
12. Get assistance whenever you need it.
13. Do not deal in fantasy and fiction, only in fact.
14. Do not start rumors by answering questions that you do not have the answer for. Rather, just tell people you do not have the answer, and when one becomes available, they will be the first to know.
15. Provide factual, timely, current information as often as possible.
16. Spotlight the small victories throughout the rightsizing process.
17. Always maintain your accountability as a leader by answering questions, getting involved with employees' worklife, and trying to have one small conversation with each employee every day.
18. Do not attempt or expect to be superhuman or perfect in the process, because you will not be—and you will only be setting yourself up for failure. Being human is good enough, and all that can be expected of you during this process.
19. Never become overcritical of yourself, the organization, or the rightsizing process—your staff will pick up on this, and it will lead to an erosion of morale.
20. Make sure to relax and use whatever stress reduction methods you can, particularly during the rightsizing process.
21. Keep all of the lines of communication open with everyone throughout the process.
22. Look to do something extra at any time, perhaps in helping an outplaced individual with a résumé, or writing a reference at the right time for someone who has been dismissed.
23. Be yourself, as people will look to you to see if you have any significant behavioral change during the rightsizing process.

The rightsizing process, as we have seen throughout this chapter, is one in which leadership—at every level of the organization, from the executive suite to the team leader's cubicle—offers the best way to a minimally-destructive and maximally-effective organizational endeavor. The process must be efficient, effective, and humanistic. The defining ethics we have described throughout this chapter are almost more important than the managerial practicums, as the healthcare business is truly "the people business" and human interaction is, and always will be, the prevailing indicator of success. Therefore, a manager faced with the emotionally laden responsibility of rightsizing can find solace and strength in the fact that a value-driven rightsizing effort guided by the collective goodwill and intelligent implementation of an organization can empower and encourage the organization toward a progressive reconstruction and vibrant renewal.

RECONSTRUCTION STRATEGY

O rganizational reconstruction, especially in healthcare, is an intricate process, the intent of which is not only to determine a new organizational structure but, perhaps more importantly, to establish a framework for the institution's new direction, mission, and future progress. Reconstruction can take place immediately after downsizing and become an integral part of organizational renewal.

Reconstruction is centered on the reorganization of the healthcare organization into a future-oriented, progressively developed service entity and is based on the strength of organizational commitment at every level. Without such commitment reconstruction is likely to be ineffective. Support for the new organizational model must be demonstrated by every employee, and its value must be recognized by every stakeholder.

In this chapter, we will examine the various strategies necessary for successful reconstruction. We will:

- discuss how to identify the need for organizational restructuring;
- review specific standards for organizational reconstruction;
- discuss approaches for gathering information critical to reconstruction planning; and
- present a specific strategic reconstruction plan.

Furthermore, we will discuss the important responsibilities and roles to be fulfilled by managers to ensure successful organizational reconstruction.

Examining the Need for Organizational Reconstruction

The needs for reconstruction are multiple and are existent throughout the organization. The entire healthcare organization must be scrutinized when identifying what should be reconstructed. Throughout this section, we will appraise a number of factors that mandate organizational reconstruction and should be used not only when forming the reconstruction plan but also when seeking support for that plan.

The most important considerations when evaluating the need for reconstruction are customer/patient needs, expectations, and current levels of satisfaction. As we have discussed elsewhere in this text, American healthcare is in a rapid state of change, which extends to payment practices, a demand for new and more valuable services, and a fear of a potential breach of the trust existing between a healthcare organization and its constituents. This last factor is perhaps the most cogent argument in favor of organizational reconstruction.

The fear of the typical American customer/patient extends to the types of services that might be available and the ability to pay for them. Even while being bombarded by media and advertising images of new services and inventive medical technology, the customer/patient is questioning the ability of the local provider to provide traditional services as well as new ones. As an organization examines the need to reconstruct itself, it must ascertain which model best offers the customer/patient good, accessible services.

To do this, the healthcare organization should conduct an exhaustive review of the utilization of various services it offers, and assign quantitative measures, based on percentages and numbers, relative to the use of those services. If, for example, an organization recognizes that some "traditional" inpatient services are no longer being utilized at a high level, but more outpatient services are being used, it should adopt a reconstruction model that allows it to more ably provide the outpatient services.

However, community perception is an important factor in the analysis of the need for reconstruction. For example, if a local community hospital is well known for pediatric services, although these services have experienced a quantitative decline in recent years, the hospital may put quality first and keep those services. That is, the perception of trust between the healthcare provider and its constituents, and the reinforcement of that trust, should be the most important factor when considering reconstruction, not strict quantitative indicators.

This notion also extends to the organization. The nebulous quality of morale, best defined as the institution's collective motivation, must be closely scrutinized during the reconstruction process. In many healthcare organizations, morale is directly linked to the organization's financial success. Put bluntly, most healthcare employees recognize the relative financial strength of their employer. If the organization is doing well financially, an assumption is made that admissions are up, services are being provided, and all personnel within the organization are fully employed. Conversely, when profits and other financial indicators are down, staff assumes that the organization is in trouble, and job security might be at stake. While this is a simplistic view (recall the discussion of the mandates for rightsizing in Chapter 1), this general perception relates directly to morale when considering reconstruction.

These four objectives should be stressed to keep morale high:

1. The reconstruction will help us be more productive in our daily work.
2. The reconstruction will make the organization more profitable.
3. The reorganization will help us achieve personal and professional goals within our individual job roles more efficiently.
4. The reconstruction will allow us to grow and prosper in pace with our surrounding community.

Because most employees are members of the community served by the healthcare organization, it is impossible to separate community perception from morale when considering reconstruction. Hence, the institution must make a strong argument in favor of the reconstruction to its employees to ensure they will advocate it to their community.

Efficiency and effectiveness are two elements that should be incorporated when identifying the need for reconstruction (Drucker 1982). The organization's relative effectiveness—the quality of the services it provides and the care it renders—should be first measured, and then opportunities must be identified that enhance current performance. For example, will the reconstruction allow the organization to increase the quality of neonatal care? Will the cost efficiency of the radiology department be positively enhanced by the reconstructed organization? In short, the need for greater efficiency and effectiveness must be at the root of the reconstruction effort.

Business development is a time-honored industrial precept that has only recently been openly discussed in healthcare (Coddington and Moore 1987). Business development, loosely defined, entails creating new profits for an organization by either expanding existing services or creating new ones. Both elements of this definition apply to the concept of reconstruction, the need for which can be premised on the demand to expand existing services—particularly the profitable ones—or could reflect an increase in demand within the customer/patient business arena. A good example of this would be the expanding need for mental health services in almost every region of North America. Similarly, a need for new services—such as gambling addiction treatment—can be included as part of a new, reconstructed organization. Business development efforts should be linked to areas that will provide increased:

- profits;
- community access;
- future potential business development;
- use of existing organizational resources;
- use of emerging organizational resources;
- exposure and credibility within the community; and
- expansion into new geographical regions.

The notion of patient access extends beyond business development. The reconstructed organization must make every effort, from the needs-analysis phase of the reconstruction plan through the actual reconstruction—to increase patient access to the organization. Accordingly, by reviewing current levels of patient access and, more importantly, by identifying areas that will increase it, the healthcare organization does not only set up a logical premise for reconstruction but establishes an important strategic business imperative.

Finally, the desire to escalate and increase services that have been both traditionally successful and recently essential should be at the vanguard of the reconstruction needs-analysis. For example, most sociologists maintain that a "second baby boom" is taking place in the United States during the 1990s. As a result, many healthcare organizations have rededicated their organizations to all phases of maternity services. After extensive analysis of current trends, specific increases, and other indicators reflected in Figure 4.1, the healthcare organization can conduct an adequate investigation that will help determine the type of reconstruction needed and specific reasons for it, and then set an initial direction for the entire reconstruction process.

Standards for Reconstruction

As we have discussed, the reconstruction plan must be realistic, logical, and value driven in order to gain commitment from the organization. In this section, we will review the standards essential to a reconstruction process to make it viable, as well as practical, in the perception of both stakeholders and staff.

Figure 4.1 Indicators to Consider When Planning Reconstruction Performance

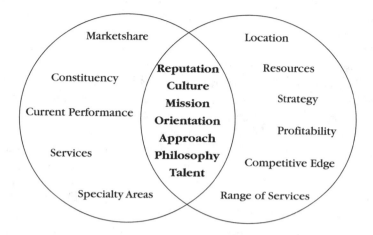

Above all, the reconstruction process must be "patient-positive." That is, the plan must address the prevalent needs and expectations of the patient populace in order to be well received, lasting, and progressive. To achieve this, the organization must have a sound awareness of patient expectations, realistically understand the current needs of the patient, and, furthermore, have a useful perspective on the patients' prominent future needs. This can be achieved through a variety of methods, which will be explained in the next section of this chapter. From the outset of the reconstruction process, however, the need to take better care of the patient should be the most important consideration in the planning process, and without question, the highest objective of the reconstruction. Because most healthcare professionals are motivated in their daily activities by providing the best care for the patient, most staff will support the "patient-positive" stance of the reconstruction plan.

The reconstruction process must also be user friendly. Many organizations have created problems by making the entire process too complex, which can occur when the reconstruction model is difficult to understand. As we discussed in the previous section, if the need for reconstruction is not explicitly explained to all organizational members, it naturally follows that there will be a lack of acceptance and dearth of commitment. Additionally, fear of the unknown—as we have discussed throughout the book—is a major element in the collective psyche of members of an organization undergoing change. When the reconstruction model is poorly presented and the reasons for it are not fully delineated, fear can strangle progress.

When undergoing reconstruction, the organization must ensure that all staff members understand their job roles within the new model, their departmental missions relative to that model, and its rudimentary dynamics relative to its ability to deliver patient services. This can be achieved by comprehensive communication using a number of strategies (Lombardi 1996). The overriding consideration in making a reconstruction as easy as possible is that the model being implemented does indeed make the staff's worklife easier. The increases in efficiency and effectiveness must be clearly displayed and understood by a majority of staff, who must also readily understand all terms, vocabulary, titles, role definitions, and other such aspects of the reconstruction process.

For instance, many healthcare organizations have ventured into a product-line reconstruction model, one of five prominent models currently being used by healthcare organizations, as will be discussed. Like the other four models, the product-line model has both strengths and relative weaknesses, depending on the institution's needs. However, in many organizations, the word "product" is still a dirty word. It can easily have a connotation that healthcare and medical services are merely "products" and that patients are simply "customers." This is an anathema to many healthcare professionals, who consider their profession a sacred trust. For example if not properly educated to what the product-line model really is, staff members can make an assortment of inaccurate perceptions and incorrect assumptions—and suffer from poor morale—simply because that model was not properly presented and implemented.

This example also demonstrates the need for comprehensive communication throughout the reconstruction process. As a standard, communication concerning the reconstruction process should be clear, concise, and as comprehensive as possible. Communication in this regard extends to not only the presentation of a new plan, but in listening and gathering data necessary to innovating the plan. To use the example of product-line models again, it is the responsibility of the organization not only to ascertain whether product-line reconstruction is necessary but also if that model can be tailored specifically to the organization. Furthermore, would the product-line model meet the specific needs of individual jobs, departmental objectives, and overall organizational initiatives? As is often the case in healthcare organizational action, communication is the key to success only if it goes both ways between staff and management, encompassing presentation as well as listening.

Another standard for the reconstruction process is that of talent maximization. Within an organization, certain departments contribute particular expertise to the overall mission. In planning for reconstruction, the healthcare organization should examine each segment of the organization, understand where specific pockets of expertise exist, and consider the best way to maximize that talent relative to the model for reconstruction, as well as the reconstruction process itself.

An often-overlooked standard for reconstruction is that of common sense. Unfortunately, many healthcare organizations use a reconstruction model simply because it is in fashion. In fact, some consultants have advocated that *all* healthcare organizations should use *one* model. This has not elicited much support from the healthcare sector, as the needs of a rural clinic in West Texas, for example are quite different from a major metropolitan medical center in Houston, an example that is true across the country. Some healthcare executives, however, still like to follow the fad, adopting the healthcare model currently in vogue instead of a more logical model, which would make more sense to both the organization and its members.

To ensure that the new organizational model makes sense, the healthcare executive should ask five basic questions:

1. Will the new model allow the majority of employees to do their job with less stress, unnecessary pressure, and undue strain?
2. Will the new model allow us to provide as many services as possible to as many people as possible efficiently?
3. Would the average employee understand this model, and think that it was a good idea?
4. Will the average patient understand this model, and recognize it as a good-faith attempt to provide better services more efficiently and effectively?
5. Does the overall plan "make sense" to me relative to emerging business directions, current trends, and past community traditions?

In many cases, the best organizational model for reconstruction is based on eminent needs, which could include poor financial performance, the increase of a specific patient population, or the overstaffing of a healthcare organization created inadvertently by a shift from inpatient care to outpatient care. Generally, eminent needs are addressed through the rightsizing process as well as the reconstruction process. In this sense, the reconstruction process should be the next step of the rightsizing process. For example, if a hospital is in fact overstaffed, the first logical step is to reduce positions that are not fully utilized—as we discussed earlier—and then immediately investigate opportunities to utilize the remaining staff fully through reconstruction.

Eminent needs are understood clearly by all members of the organization. Most employees quickly recognize when a hospital is losing money, or when the census is down. Therefore, another standard for reconstruction is getting all staff members to participate in the reconstruction process. Because all staff members can—ideally—recognize the need to rightsize and reconstruct, they should also be held accountable to provide suggestions to help the organization transform into a viable, future-oriented entity. If staff members are not included in reconstruction plans, they will not participate in the plan once formulated and will furthermore harbor justifiable resentment to the organization for "dictating" a new plan that does not take into account their expert input.

Eliciting sound input from staff members allows an institution to get feedback about the process from the "superstar" and "steady" employees, who are the backbone of any successful healthcare organization. In fact, any restructuring must remotivate these key employees. The reconstruction effort should be seen as a reward for the organizational process of rightsizing. That is, because the organization made the "tough call" and rightsized to maintain stability, the reconstruction should be presented as an opportunity to prepare to "thrive," not merely "survive." If done successfully, rightsizing preserves the employment of the "superstar" and "steady" employees and ideally removes the effect, if not the employment, of the "nonplayers." Participating in discussions concerning the new organizational model—and the entire reconstruction process itself—motivates the solid performers as they realize they are being asked to contribute to the new direction of their institution.

As such, the reconstruction effort becomes a focal point, which should take the place of the previous one—the rightsizing. Fundamentally, the organization is now shifting from a negative circumstance—the rightsizing—to a positive one—the reconstruction. By sharing the opportunity to make plans for the new organization, provide input for specific directions, and render insights that will help construct the new organization, it is clearly expressing to its committed employees its desire to move toward "total organizational leadership" where everyone will be a leader and the organization will focus on the future, not the past.

Organizational motivation is greatly enhanced when these additional factors are also considered:

- The organization must ensure that the reasons for reconstruction are clearly stated, constantly referred to, and specifically delineated throughout the process.
- Direct community benefits, such as improvement of services, greater

access to those services, and other notable improvements should be publicized throughout the process.

- The reconstruction process, above all else, must not compromise patient service in any manner. Even a *perceived* lack of service can be devastating to the entire reconstruction process. Accordingly, it is essential to separate fact from fiction when breaches in patient service are cited, but more importantly, every consideration must be placed toward not only maintaining, but indeed upgrading, patient services. This is not only essential to motivation, but essential to the entire reconstruction process.

- The reconstruction process must be proactively planned, and with the greatest acuity possible all potential problems and confounding issues must be anticipated, addressed, and resolved before the process takes place.

- The reconstructing facility must take advantage of "natural opportunities" to improve its services and provide better care. For example, if there is a natural surge in the number of outpatient cases, the organization that adopts an organizational reconstruction model that stresses and enhances such outpatient services is simply "doing what comes naturally." The majority of employees will recognize this, and it can be demonstrated as a "quick win" that will ensure future success.

- If the organization's reconstruction plan is strategically sound, keeps pace with change in the community, improves quality of service, demonstrates community benefit, and is seen as being value-driven as well as doing good business, the reconstruction effort will not only be motivating, it will be effective.

The last standard for reconstruction is that, to be accepted and effective, it must maintain the organization's mission and overall philosophy. Under no condition should the institution's essential mission—as being a people-oriented, value-driven human services community trust—be compromised. As an example, certain healthcare organizations have made the mistake of rightsizing to facilitate a reconstruction. Unfortunately, the rightsizing took place across the employee ranks, while the organization retained fourteen vice presidential slots. It becomes a difficult proposition for the organization to convince its employees that it has "rightsized the right way" to achieve a more progressive organizational model, particularly if a number of staff believe that half of the vice presidential postions could have easily been eliminated.

The healthcare organization should instead hold as the prevailing standard the objective of realizing that the basic mission has not changed but conditions in the marketplace and the community have indeed altered. As a result, in order to maintain the integrity of the mission, reconstruction is necessary. However, the reconstruction—as is the case with all organizational action—holds as its basic precept the unwavering commitment of providing better services for more community members in a progressive, quality-conscious, value-driven manner at all times. Reconstruction therefore is simply an attempt to meet more fully this all-important mission.

Information Collection Methods

To select the appropriate model for reconstruction, the organization must first understand clearly its community environment, marketplace dynamics, organizational issues, and other essential information that is at the root of enlightened strategic planning. In this section, we will outline a variety of techniques to collect essential information from the customer/patient community, the overall organization, individual groups and departments, and specific job role components. Healthcare organizations undergoing the reconstruction process should use a number of these techniques—based on comfort, applicability, and appropriateness—to select an accurate reconstruction model and strategy.

As an initial strategy, many healthcare organizations have found great value in forming a *reconstruction committee*, the purpose of which is to identify specific trends affecting the institution and to make suggestions about the type of reconstruction model to use. In some organizations, this committee has been composed of managers, skilled professionals, and "business-oriented" supervisors who understand the fiscal implications of reconstruction. Other organizations use a hybrid committee consisting of both employees and managers. This type of committee can provide a wealth of viewpoints about organizational action in addition to specific financial and business concerns.

Both types of committees have drawbacks relative to their membership. In the first type, input is usually directed toward business and financial conditions, but the "human element," specifically as it relates to the "average working stiff," can be lost. But the second committee might lack business acumen, and thus certain recommendations might be "overruled" because of prevailing business conditions. As a result, a combination approach is suggested: The reconstruction committee should have a total membership of twelve individuals. Four of these individuals would be nonexempt employees representing various sectors of the healthcare organization. The only requirement is that these individuals are established performers at the "superstar" level. There is no need to include "chronic nonplayers." Rather than a democratic process, the reconstruction process is a business process with the humane intent of optimizing the healthcare organization's future in the community and not a forum for "nonplayers" to air their grievances.

Another four members of the reconstruction committee would consist of supervisors and managers from across the organization. Once again, these individuals would be proven performers at the "superstar" level; at least two of these four members should be skilled in finance, business development, community relations, and other applicable areas vital to a reconstruction plan.

The final four members should consist of a physician, a volunteer member, a senior executive, and an at-large member—perhaps the CEO, a board member, or anyone else who meets these following criteria:

- willingness to participate in the reconstruction effort;
- credible experience within their technical field;
- credible tenure with the organization;
- a positive, well-motivated commitment to the organization;
- the ability to network with counterparts at other hospitals and healthcare organizations;
- excellent communication skills; and
- great listening skills.

These last two requirements are essential. Members of the reconstruction committee should be held accountable for spreading its results and, more importantly, presenting any viewpoints, opinions, and perspectives they hear and see. Essentially, members of the reconstruction committee operate not only as participants in community discussions but as conduits to their counterparts throughout the organization about the reconstruction process.

In summary, the reconstruction committee must:

1. collect and provide essential information that will help formulate the reconstruction plan;
2. compose in a timely fashion—usually within three months—a suggested plan for reconstruction; and
3. help management implement the reconstruction process.

The committee can be greatly assisted by using *direct patient input*, which can be gathered in a variety of methods. In some institutions, questionnaires are used to identify relative patient satisfaction (Lombardi 1996). Patient InfoCards, visitor questionnaires, and patient surveys provide essential feedback that should be incorporated when forming a reconstruction plan. Certainly, as we have discussed, utilization charting, billing practices, and other traditional indicators of patient access, usage, and demand are very useful.

Additionally, in recent years, several other techniques have garnered specific patient input. One practice is the use of *focus groups*, which have been used for years by Fortune 500 companies, particularly by marketing departments, to determine the feasibility of new products, as well as upgrading existing products. This two-part objective applies well to the healthcare organization undergoing reconstruction. Ideally, the organization should invite a focus group of fifteen community members to the institution for a welcoming presentation by the CEO, a well-catered lunch, and a general discussion about the healthcare organization's plans; the group should then be invited to discuss their satisfaction with current products and services, as well as their additional future needs.

Consider the advantage gained by a small Midwestern hospital in using focus groups. In establishing the group, fifteen "typical" residents of the outlying small community were invited to the healthcare organization for a luncheon. While discussing present trends, no significant information was revealed to the organization. However, as future trends were discussed, one individual in the community—a retired high school teacher—mentioned the upcoming closing of one of the community's two high schools. This, she explained, was because "Many of the kids who go to school here go away to college and don't come back!" On further questioning, members of the reconstruction committee—three of whom were facilitating the focus group—concluded that the hospital's future direction should be geared toward handling the "age wave"; they therefore recommended a reconstruction plan that would accommodate their community's major population of retirees and other "golden-agers."

Three considerations are essential when using a focus group. First, no focus group is an accurate representation of the entire community, and as such, it should be seen as an opportunity to gather some general perceptions, some revelation, and, ideally, some validation of the plans the organization has already conceived. Second, focus groups should center on two or three specific issues—in cases of reconstruction, they should focus only on present trends and future demands. Focus groups are anything but "focused," and as a result, their discussions can often become unwieldy, misdirected, and subjectively inaccurate. Finally, members of the focus group must be well managed in their interaction, particularly when discussing reconstruction, where fear could easily be generated. For example, if a focus group at a local community hospital is told, "We just finished rightsizing, and now we're trying to figure out how to reconstruct ourselves," the focus group can naturally assume that the hospital has empowered fifteen community members to start unfounded rumors about the hospital's imminent demise!

The participation of *board members* can also be useful when making reconstruction plans, and many community hospitals have used board retreats as an opportunity to seek guidance on reconstruction. Certainly, it might be politically expedient—as well as organizationally effective—to have a reconstruction plan prepared, at least conceptually, prior to presenting it to the board. However, the participation of certain board members on the reconstruction committee—or using a separate committee consisting exclusively of four or five board members working in concert with the reconstruction committee—can be useful in both forming the reconstruction plan as well as implementing it.

Another information-gathering tool is the *organizational audit*, which can be conducted in several ways. In some institutions, an organizational psychologist has discussed specific issues with managers as well as employees, which has proved helpful. In other cases, using a checklist, such as the one illustrated in Figure 4.2, which is sent to all employees and then collated, has been useful. The author uses this checklist when consulting healthcare institutions, and it can provide an effective way to begin discussions with staff about the reconstruction process. Fundamentally, the checklist *asks* for input. The employee cannot "assume" that the organization "knows"—either organizationally, telepathically, or by other means—that natural opportunities exist and what individual considerations should be made in the interests of a progressive reconstruction and transformation process.

Figure 4.2   Checklist for Management Audit

Current Year Review Considerations

1. Cite Major Team/Group Achievements
2. Stress Areas of Marked, Quantifiable Improvement over Previous Year
3. Indicate Contribution Value to the Organization
4. Consider Relevance to Customer/Patient
5. Note Outstanding Individual Action and Accomplishment
6. Incorporate Any Subgroup or "Smaller Team" Contribution
7. Record Recognizable, Tangible Results and Outcomes
8. Identify Intangible Benefits and Values to the Group, Organization and Patient
9. Assess Long-Term Value and Significance to Organizational "Mutual Benefit"
10. Recognize Quantitative Nature of Goal Accomplishment
11. Appraise Qualitative Nature of Goal Attainment
12. Group Pride, Morale, Affiliation, and Satisfaction Should Result from This Recognition
13. Minimum of Six Entries
14. Maximum of Twelve Entries
15. All Member Contribution Should Be Considered in Overall Assessment

Audits can also extend to *departmental reviews*, where these considerations are reviewed and analyzed:

- current optimization and utilization of the department;
- future trends within the specific technical area of the department services;
- specific trends within the department's technical community, for example, national trends for psychiatric social workers, national trends for registered dieticians, etc.;
- specific customer/patient relevance within the community for the department's services. For example, a maternity ward in a community hospital in the Bronx, New York, would be utilized at a higher level than a maternity ward in Sun City, Arizona;
- specific customer/patient feedback presented to the department regarding not only its services specifically, but also feedback relative to the organization's overall performance as suggested by customer/patient comments; and
- the specific leadership of the department, and its commitment to participating in a reconstructed organization.

This last point merits further discussion. In many healthcare organizations, unfortunately, certain departments have built "turfs" and "fiefdoms." When reconstruction occurs, the individuals who have created these somewhat self-absorbed entities become naturally threatened. In some cases, these individuals might hinder the reconstruction process, even though their departmental members are quite enthusiastic about it. These sentiments can only be recognized if a departmental audit is conducted in concert with other methods. Without this audit, the manager's impressions and perceptions presented as the sole answer to the above questions comprising a departmental audit, when in reality, it might simply be the individual perceptions of a leader who is not particularly "with the program."

Finally, conducting an *organizational survey* can be well-timed between an institution's rightsizing process and its reconstruction (Lombardi 1994). An organizational survey, such as the Health Organizational Survey System, can present a wide spectrum of critical information that is not only specific to the reconstruction effort but also educational about the prevailing morale within the organization, required managerial action, and other dimensions essential to reconstruction. Once again, if individuals are asked for their opinion, particularly under the aegis of a confidential, professional survey, they will be more willing to venture their opinions and perspectives than if they are not asked.

Gathering intelligence effectively throughout a healthcare organization should be continuous, regardless of whether the organization is undergoing reconstruction. However, in times of reconstruction, it is absolutely vital for the healthcare organization to obtain as much information as possible about forming an appropriate reconstruction plan. By following the guidance of a well-structured reconstruction committee, and employing at least a majority of the techniques suggested in this section, the healthcare organization can be better prepared to form a reconstruction plan.

Forming the Reconstruction Plan

Forming the reconstruction plan is relatively easy, as it is premised on the needs analysis review, action standards, and intelligence-gathering processes that we have discussed. Once the organization has addressed these specific action standards, conducted a proper needs analysis review, and gathered as much input as possible about reconstruction plans, forming the plan takes several simple steps.

To begin with, the organization must determine what type of reconstruction model to use. This should be based on apparent needs and the organization's specific nuances. In the next chapter, we will not only discuss the most prominent, effective reconstruction models, but we will begin the discussion in Chapter 5 with a comprehensive discussion on selecting the proper organizational model.

Notwithstanding the selection of an adequate organizational model, the reconstruction plan takes shape most clearly with the use of a timeline plan, as suggested by Figure 4.3. As is the case with the rightsizing process, the reconstruction plan must be concise, timely, and comprehensive. For example, the reconstruction committee should have three months to complete its work and achieve their three basic objectives. Likewise, a comprehensive organizational reconstruction plan should achieve four objectives:

1. to identify the specific time frame for reconstruction;
2. to assign responsibilities for reconstructive action;
3. to identify which departments will be affected by the

Figure 4.3 Sample Timeline

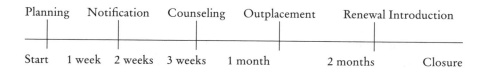

reconstruction, which individuals who will be affected, and which individuals in departments will be unaffected; and

4. to gather pertinent, specific information about implementing the reconstruction, future action, reconstruction model features, and other essential information.

The reconstruction plan must have a finite time frame. Usually, the reconstruction process should take approximately six months. For example, the reconstruction committee should be allowed to begin and complete its work within the first three months of this six-month sequence, and every attempt should be made by the hierarchy to communicate specific information about the reconstruction plan during this time. Furthermore, all managers should extend their communication responsibilities to all members of their staff, collecting important input as well as spreading essential information. Implicit in this six-month sequence is the fact that the rightsizing process has occurred prior, not simultaneous, to the reconstruction, as has already been discussed.

Throughout the six-month sequence, the benefits of the reconstruction should be grouped into three or four major "talking points," which can usually be described as greater patient service, greater probability for future success, the extension of greater patient access and increased/better services, and an organizational structure to allow greater individual and professional achievement. These points should be stressed in formal organizational communication; advocated by every department, supervisor and team leader; and added to input from "superstar" and "steady" organizational members.

From a humanistic and business standpoint, individuals who are directly affected by the reconstruction should be given greater consideration in the reconstruction process than unaffected individuals. This does not mean, of course, that management should ignore those staff members who are not directly affected: Reconstruction affects *everyone*—simply because everyone is a member of an organization undergoing change.

It is essential, however, for the institution to extend special consideration to individuals whose departments are being reorganized, whose job descriptions are being redefined, or whose role in the organization is being reinvented. During the actual reconstruction process, and the establishment of the plan, special meetings should be scheduled to address the specific concerns of these individuals. These forums can include sessions in which job descriptions are rewritten; individual action is reassessed; and suggestion and comment is continuously elicited, encouraged, engaged, and used when appropriate.

In addition to a general timeline for the entire organization, a specific timeline might be generated for each department listing specific guidelines, strategies, and approaches to the reconstruction clearly identified to the employees. Constructing a specific departmental plan provides clarity to the individual employee, extends reassurance about job security and stability, negates rumors and conjecture, and provides a clear direction for the individual's job scope or departmental action.

Many facets of the reconstruction plan depend on the reconstruction model the organization adopts. At this point, it is vital to understand that several components can be incorporated into that reconstruction plan, depending on the institution's particular needs and strategic inclinations. The compenents include:

- specific locations and departments that the reorganization and reconstruction might affect;
- specific "checkpoints" to gauge the success of the reconstruction plan;
- important community events, such as open houses and other community-based interactions, that will help promote the reconstruction; and
- new names, titles, or "labels" that will assist in the introduction of the reconstruction plan.

In all cases, it is important for the reconstruction plan to be published widely throughout the organization. This has been accomplished in some organizations by circulating a booklet to all staff members that describes the timeline and other parts of the reconstruction plan. In other healthcare organizations, the plan has been described in a "payroll envelope stuffer" delivered to employees when they receive their regular paycheck—an excellent time to hear from their employer. In other cases, the reconstruction plan has been part of an annual report.

Regardless of the technique used, the reconstruction plan must be distributed to all employees. It has to be short and concise, and must contain the essential information described here. Without such a publication, the organization increases the likelihood that rumor will take the place of communication, fiction may take the place of fact.

Leadership Roles and Responsibilities During Reconstruction

Throughout the entire reconstruction process several roles must be fulfilled by leaders throughout the organization. To begin with, every leader—whether a senior executive, middle-line manager, supervisor, or team leader—must operate as an *organizational advocate*. Principally, leaders at every level must embrace the reconstruction plan as *our* plan and not just the "CEO's plan" or, worse, "their" plan. The leader must use the "talking points" when describing the benefits of the reconstruction plan, and its overarching objective of improving the healthcare organization.

The leader must be an *innovator* in the reconstruction process. Despite the most well-intentioned plans, the process will "hit a few snags" in its implementation. Accordingly, each leader must recognize problems as they occur, immediately formulate a solution to those problems in concert with his or her staff members, and use ingenuity to help the process along. A leader who immediately blames a failure in the reconstruction process on "them" or "this process" is someone who is abdicating his or her role as a leader. Obviously, if a problem that requires executive intervention occurs, the leader must possess the valor necessary to elicit assistance from the senior executive, and make the corrections necessary to complete the process successfully.

Throughout the process, the leader must be a *technical expert*. As a new model for the organization takes hold, the individual department head or team leader must ensure that all technical requirements are being met by his or her department. In fact, technical services should be enhanced by the reconstruction process. Additionally, any technical questions that might arise should be answered by departmental leaders in their respective departments, and each individual manager should operate as an internal consultant to the organization on technical matters. This responsibility begins at the outset of the reconstruction process and continues prominently through the reconstruction and renewal stages of organizational transformation.

Healthcare leaders must be at their *interpersonal best* during the reconstruction effort. That is, their entire assortment of interpersonal abilities must be summoned to meet the challenges of reconstruction. In this regard, the healthcare leader must be open to suggestions, opinions, and anything else that might help the process. The healthcare leader must be accessible to all subordinate staff members to handle concerns, fear, and questions regarding the process and the organization's "new direction." The leader must be a *voice of reason* and be sensible when dealing with others. This involves acting appropriately in times of crisis, balancing his or her emotions with a resolute commitment to making the process successful. Above all else, the healthcare leader must use the pronoun "we" when dealing with staff to negate the unintentional but nefarious impact of the pronouns "us" and "they." As we have discussed, no "us" and "they" exist in modern healthcare—rather, the community, organization, individual departments, and each employee comprises a greater, larger "we."

The healthcare leader must be a *participant* throughout the entire process, which involves participating in various action planning and in chain-of-command discussions with immediate supervisors and organizational hierarchy. Leaders must certainly participate in building the cooperation, commitment, and support of their staff members. Without this support, the process is doomed. The individual manager is the most important catalytic agent during the reconstruction process, and accordingly, he or she must participate from the beginning to the successful conclusion. Without the individual manager and supervisor leading the process—being positive, committed, focused on solutions instead of problems, and value-driven—a reconstruction process will not succeed.

Implementing Reconstruction by Communication

As indicated by the reorganization plan timeline, the organization will implement its new structure on a certain date. This implementation can usually be celebrated by a new title for the organization, a major introduction event, or any other suitable way to introduce the new system. With the proper planning, and specific implementation of the models discussed in the next chapter, the reconstruction effort can be implemented, provided employees understand their new role in the reconstructed organization, the intent of the new model, and the explicit benefits of moving to a new organizational model.

A specific set of communication tools should be established to implement the reconstruction process, including formal presentations, conducted by the CEO, dealing with the details of the reconstruction effort, the implementation of the model, and the resolution of key concerns and organizational issues.

Specific forums can be planned in which the reconstruction effort is described to community members, members of the board of directors, staff members, volunteer groups, and other stakeholders in the healthcare organization. Furthermore, informal communication devices, such as "lunch with the CEO," "town hall meetings," and other interactive sessions should be used.

Normal communication avenues within the organization should be used at their highest possible level. Individual departmental managers who normally conduct monthly meetings with their staff should now make their meetings weekly. E-mail messages, sent to organizational members on a daily basis, should take on a special flavor, specifically when they relate to the reconstruction process. Many times, the use of a "hook" can be useful in the reconstruction process. For example, some healthcare organizations use renewal strategies, such as *Healthcare 2000* and other such names, as themes for their entire reorganization efforts, from rightsizing to renewal. This is not only a useful focal device, but it also helps distinguish important communication about the reconstruction from "routine" communication. For example, any e-mail relating to the *Healthcare 2000* initiative would be sent under the title "HC-2000." In other institutions, new "organizational colors," such as teal, aqua, or other "nouveau" hues have been used to represent an organizational initiative. As elemental as it might seem, an organization using *Healthcare 2000* as a reconstruction label, replete with information distributed on aqua paper, provides a user-friendly way to emphasize that the organization is taking change seriously.

Finally, ten communication rules must be employed by the healthcare organization to ensure that the reconstruction process will be effective, value-driven, and efficient:

1. The benefits of the reconstruction must be identified clearly and communicated on a daily basis throughout the reconstruction effort.

2. While "fine tuning" is allowed throughout the reconstruction process, no "second guessing" is allowed, particularly by managers in public view of their staff.

3. Special consideration should be given to "superstars" and "steady" players in any communication forum throughout the reconstruction process.

4. Any "nonplayer" who did not get the message to improve performance after the rightsizing should be closely monitored throughout the reconstruction process to ensure their penchant for creating rumors, conjecture, and gossip does not subvert workplace communication.

5. All members of the organization must be encouraged to participate in the reconstruction process, and not act merely as spectators.

6. Any benefits immediately gained in the reconstruction process—particularly those that relate to patient service—should be highlighted throughout the organization, using newsletters, CEO letters, and other appropriate communication organs.

7. The reconstruction process should be highlighted as "investment-driven"—that is, the investment made by the time, energy, and commitment of each stakeholder—notably that of each and every employee—is held in the highest importance.

8. Achievements along the timeline plan for reconstruction should be highlighted throughout the process; special events, such as

pizza parties, luncheons, and other rewards, should be provided to facilitate reconstruction momentum.

9. "Defining moments," such as formal letters from patients to the CEO and other "fan mail" that are direct results of the reconstruction, should be publicized and used as examples of the value of reconstruction.

10. All action during the reconstruction must be "value-driven"—to reflect the values of decency, fortitude, industry, integrity, and knowledge—as well as "valor-driven"—to reflect the encouragement, interpersonal support, and "patient-positive focus" produced by the majority of staff members.

As we discussed in the introduction of this chapter, the reconstruction process can be an intricate organizational endeavor, with perilous risks and potential organizational derailment. However, with progressive planning, clear communication, and strong stakeholder investment from all organizational participants, the reconstruction process can become positive, humanistic, and, ultimately, advantageous to both the organization and the customer/patient.

References

Coddington, D. C., and K. D. Moore. 1987. *Market-Driven Strategies in Health Care*. San Francisco: Jossey-Bass.

Drucker, P. F. 1982. *The Changing World of the Executive*. New York: Times Books.

Lombardi, D. N. 1994. *The Healthcare Organizational Survey System*. Chicago: American Hospital Publishing.

———. 1996. *Thriving in an Age of Change*. Chicago: Health Administration Press.

IMPLEMENTING A NEW STRUCTURE

As we have discussed, the reconstruction process is fraught with apprehension, change, and fear for all members of a healthcare organization. Accordingly, the process must be implemented with clarity, direction, and a sense of positivity. In addition to the strategies described in the previous chapter, the selection of a new organizational model is an essential component of reconstruction and renewal.

In this chapter, we will review the five most prominent models for healthcare reorganization and reconstruction:

- the product-line model;
- the action-line model;
- the decentralized-decision model;
- the triad model; and
- the traditional organizational model.

In addition to reviewing each model and its relevant strengths and benefits, the specific features of each will be delineated and fully described. Moreover, the respective ability of each model to motivate, recommit staff, and facilitate future growth and progress will also be explored.

Considerations for Model Selection

Several criteria must be considered when healthcare leadership decides on a new organizational model. All too often, management will choose an organizational model simply because it is "trendy," popular, or commonly used throughout the healthcare industry. The folly of this is that healthcare organizations are becoming increasingly community oriented and patient driven, and must thus customize to meet new patient demands and increasing expectations.

Therefore, patients are the first consideration when selecting a new organizational model. Management must fully consider the types of patients who will use the organization's services, as well as the specific services that will be required. Management must then compute the most effective way to deliver those services most efficiently.

Focusing on patient needs to choose an organizational model begins with basic demographics. Such factors as the male/female composition of the service area, the age classification of the community, and other essential components must be considered. For example, in a community consisting primarily of young families, the model has to include child services, maternity services, and other similar services. Conversely, if the community population consists mainly of retirees, geriatric services must be part of the new organizational model. In both examples, the emphasis on outpatient services, which we have discussed throughout this text, will become a major factor when selecting the new model.

Three factors should be considered when reviewing a community's demographic composition. First, the current demographics in the area must be assessed and the major details of each demographic segment identified. Second, the organization must consider how it could best address the healthcare needs of those segments. Third, consideration should be given to the future growth of the community's various demographic groups. For example, if a hospital is located in the northeast United States, it must constantly assess and plan for the medical needs of various immigrant groups.

The second prevailing consideration for selecting a healthcare organizational model is the intent of the organization to become the vortex of healthcare services. A vortex, simply defined, is the center part of a whirlpool that pulls water toward the center. As suggested in Figure 5.1, the healthcare organization must act as a vortex to its community. Essentially, the new organizational model must provide a clear delineation of its services, offer easy access to those significant services, and—perhaps most often overlooked—act as a conduit to other healthcare institutions providing specialized services.

Currently, many organizations that have operated as "typical" community hospitals regard the future fearfully, as surrounding competitive hospitals offer specialized services. If the community hospital insists on being a typical community healthcare provider—that is, offering traditional services without at least trying to facilitate specialized services for its customer/patients—it is doomed for certain failure. On the other

Figure 5.1   The Healthcare Organization as a Community Vortex

hand, if a community hospital acts as a vortex for healthcare services, it can become the starting point for providing healthcare services of any kind.

Implicit to this strategy is the need to create partnerships with other organizations. Acting as a conduit for healthcare services, not only with neighboring institutions but with physician groups, clinics, homes for the aging, and other providers, is essential to an organization's success.

Becoming a healthcare conduit should be a primary feature of the new organizational model. Most staff members will adapt to change—except change for its own sake. If the new model clearly increases the institution's ability to orchestrate the delivery of healthcare services, the typical employee will be reassured that the organization can proactively provide services to its community members. With this in mind, four basic questions should be asked during the selection of the new organizational model, as well as throughout the reconstruction process:

1. What services do we currently offer?
2. What services *should* we offer?

3. What services can we offer in concert with neighboring healthcare providers?
4. Which organizational model will best clearly communicate to our community that we are now in a position to act as a conduit to other healthcare providers?

As well as becoming a conduit for healthcare services, the organization must maintain its needed services, which can be accomplished by reviewing what the organization's role has traditionally been throughout the community. Under no circumstances should any positive attribute of the institution become "lost in the shuffle" of reorganization. This promotes fear throughout the community and can certainly cause a tremendous amount of staff apprehension. Accordingly, the organization should remember that maintaining the "sources of pride" must be an integral goal of the new organizational model. For example, if a community hospital is revered throughout its community because of its efficient emergency room, maternity ward, and inpatient services, these three features should be not only maintained in the new organizational model but reemphasized as a cornerstone for the new organizational model. In short, the new model should build upon the institution's established strengths and never eviscerate the traditional role or long-term regarded attributes of the hospital.

Using the "cornerstone" role of traditional services as a starting point, the new model should emphasize the institution's new services and capabilities. For example, if a new model can incorporate the "vortex" approach of using the hospital as a referral point to specific acute care clinics, organizational strength is doubled rather than cut in half. These five questions should be asked when considering the *role definition* of the new organization and its structural model:

1. What are our traditional strengths?
2. What is our role within the community, as perceived by the customer/patient?
3. What is our traditional role, as viewed by our employees?
4. What are some specific new dimensions our institution wants to embrace with the new organizational model?
5. Given the answers to these questions, what organizational model makes the most sense for reinforcing our traditional strengths while introducing and promoting our new ones?

The overall intent and objective of reconstruction is to strengthen the healthcare organization. Accordingly, the new model should enable the institution to gain a competitive edge over its rival facilities. The most overlooked, least utilized source of power within an organization in healthcare is its "people strength." As much as healthcare executives like to laud their organizations as being "people-driven," or pride themselves on being in the "people business," fiscal disarray in a hospital's year-end report can quickly shift the emphasis and focus of executive judgment from the "people line" to the "bottom line." However, fiscal prosperity of a healthcare organization is usually found in the strength of its human resources, or across the "people line" (Lombardi 1996). Therefore, the "people-line" considerations that should be considered when selecting a new model fall into these four categories:

1. **Healthcare service skills**, to include the services provided, the organization's collective expertise, and individual talents that translate into the provision of specialized services and unique healthcare products for the service community;
2. **Management skills**, which are essential not only to the short-term implementation of a new organizational model, but in the facility's long-term growth and progress;
3. **Business skills**, to include the institution's ability to conduct itself not only as a human service entity but as a functioning business entity; and
4. **Leadership skills**, exhibited by not only nominal leaders, but by specialists, staff members, and in a real sense, *every* staff member.

The new model must empower every staff member to strive for operational effectiveness, optimum contribution to the organization, and maximum growth and development. Some organizational models can stifle all three of these essential motivating facets of healthcare worklife. Other models, as you will see throughout this chapter, can embolden them.

Closely related to the issue of "people-line" talent is the need for the new model to take maximum advantage of the organization's diversity. This includes the staff members' skills. The new model should let each staff member give the organization his or her perspectives on healthcare provision, provide insight on customer/patient expectations and allow each member to act independently and accountably within the organization's parameters. Furthermore, the new model should use each member's experience and technical knowledge—and provide him or her the chance to develop and grow in pace with the customer/patient community, the healthcare organization, and his or her respective field of endeavor.

Recently, much has been written about the healthcare organization being a "learning organization." Unfortunately, many of these depictions are quite esoteric and theoretical and have limited practical value to the healthcare practitioner. The new organizational model, however, should help the institution become self-educating and encourage all staff members to contribute to its collective knowledge base. This includes the ability to identify community trends quickly as well as trends in the provision of new services and new technology.

Moreover, the new model should easily be able to receive feedback from patient community members and, conversely, be able to deliver a unified message regarding its mission, objectives, and services to the community. The new model must be able to embrace change in a way that educates the patient, as well as its ability to identify and adapt to change within the patient community. Finally, the model selected for the newly reconstructed organization should be able to elicit as much information and knowledge as possible to change and progress in pace with its community without losing the trust and commitment of its most important constituent, the individual customer/patient.

Steps for Implementing a New Organizational Model

Following a review of the primary considerations and criteria for the selection of a new organizational model, a practical strategy should be determined by the organizational leadership to implement and refine it. There are five steps in this process.

Establish a selection committee for the new organizational model

While the executive office of a healthcare organization has the primary responsibility for selecting the new organizational model, input and specific perspectives should be collected whenever possible from all levels of the organization. As has been discussed, this can be carried out by the reconstruction committee, consisting of staff members from all levels of the institution. In other cases, only the executive leadership and management staff might be involved in the process.

Perhaps the most effective method, however, is to establish a "lead group" to select the model. After reviewing the criteria suggested in this chapter, this group—composed of five key executives from the organization—would suggest the specific model the institution should adopt. This group could use data from other institutions that adopted similar models, incorporate the feedback of various staff committees, or examine the results of the change readiness index and other survey instruments—in concert with essential marketing data—to propose the new model.

Establish an action plan for implementation

Lack of communication about the organizational model can be deadly when trying to implement it. A void in communication can result in widespread fear, trepidation, and outright resistance to the new model. As in many cases in organizational change, communication is a key component for success.

It is therefore vital that a timeline be established; this timeline must be clearly stated and delineate a specific schedule for implementation of the new model. If the organization has moved efficiently during rightsizing and the initial stages of reconstruction, planning and implementing the new model should take between three to six months.

Stress consistency of purpose

In implementing a new model, it is vital to remember the three basic stages of time. To begin with, the new organizational model should be selected and implemented with the intent of celebrating the organizaton's positive attributes and "hallmark features" that the community and staff recognized in the *past*. Second, the model should emphasize the need to address present conditions as well as *current challenges* that are emerging. Finally, the new model should anticipate the *future needs* of the patient community, which will be clearly recognized by staff. In preparing to unveil a new organizational model, the executive staff must stress this consistency of purpose in all communication.

Create support for the model

The new model must eventually be understood and supported by each staff member. This word-of-mouth support is the best form of advertising not only in healthcare marketing efforts but in generating organization-wide communication. There are two approaches to creating a sense of support during the model's initial implementation.

The first approach is to use the prototypical "chain of command" in presenting the new model: All of the executives, directors, managers, and supervisors are given a detailed presentation that describes the features of the new organizational model and how its adheres to the defining criteria listed earlier. Each manager is then given a set of guidelines and "teaching aids" to help explain to employees the benefits of the new model and how it will be implemented. This approach empowers each individual manager with the responsibility to understand the model and then to present it to individual staff members. The individual manager however, might not be fully commited to the new model, be resistant to its implementation, or feel that his or her power will somehow be lost during the transition. For example, if a manager in a traditional healthcare organization stands to lose a certain amount of supervisory responsibility when the institution adopts the product-line model, it is doubtful that he or she will enthusiastically support the new model to respective staff members.

Accordingly, the second approach allows the organization itself to present the new model and its benefits. Here, the CEO prepares a report on the new model that contains:

- an overview of the new model;
- how it will benefit the customer/patient;
- how it will benefit staff members;
- how it will preserve the organization's past strengths, meet current demands, and address future requirements of the institution; and
- an overall, "user-friendly" action plan for its full implementation.

This presentation can be part of a "CEO report" that can be distributed in booklet form throughout the organization. Additionally, the CEO can make presentations to specific groups of employees and answer questions on how the new model will affect them. This effort can be supplemented by the education department of a community hospital, for example, which can prepare a more refined presentation for use on closed-circuit television throughout the facility, at various employee meetings, or for special sessions conducted by educational professionals or consultants.

The strength of this latter approach is that it allows the CEO to become the focal point for the organizational reconstruction, it enlists the participation of every staff member, and it provides the opportunity for each employee to understand how the new model will affect his or her particular area of responsibility. The only apparent downside, in the author's consulting experience and other sources, is that some "passive aggressiveness" can be realized subsequent to the CEO's presentation. This is a small negative consideration, as a certain amount of passive aggressiveness always exists in any organization where change is taking place.

Implement the model throughout the organization

The final step is the full-scale implementation of the model, which is, in essence, a dramatic shift of the healthcare organization from one structure to a new, better one. These are the necessary steps to follow when actually implementing the model:

1. **Publish new organizational charts,** not only for the entire organization but for each particular department.

2. **Set a specific target date** for when the entire organization will shift from the old model to the new one. This date is when the organizational transition will be complete, resolute, and, after a certain amount of discussion, non-negotiable. Under no circumstances should the old organizational model be resurrected following this date, nor should the new model be revised unnecessarily or dramatically once implemented.

3. **Management support for the model** must be absolute, clear, and apparent from the initial adaptation of the new organizational model to its final installation. In the transformation process, the individual supervisor or team leader is, in a real sense, more important than the CEO. If a particular supervisor or departmental manager is not "with the program," it is difficult to expect that members of his or her department will support the new model fully. A certain amount of leadership fortitude and direction is required to ensure that managers understand they are critical components of the transformation process and that their full commitment is required if the reorganization is to succeed.

4. **Gain employee support for the new model.** If the organization has taken every stride toward ensuring that all members of the organization understand the new model, employee support will become apparent when the transition takes place. However, even with the best intentions and the most effective methods, a certain amount of employee apprehension will exist, even with well-motivated "superstar" employees. It is essential that the CEO and all managers strive to:
   - stay visible
   - listen
   - ask questions
   - answer concerns
   - explain new directions
   - show empathy
   - provide support
   - observe intently
   - perceive thoughtfully
   - maintain accountability

   throughout the entire process.

5. **Emphasis on "patient-first" focus** must be continuous, apparent, and highlighted throughout the shift to a new organizational model. After all, the entire reason for rightsizing and renewing is to better serve the customer/patient. This theme must not only be revisited but reinforced by all managers as a new organizational model takes precedent over the old model and its "old way of doing things."

By following the guidelines discussed in this section, the organization can ensure fluid and positive transition; it can also assure the customer/patient that the institution is implementing a "better way of doing things." Obviously, if the employees are fully aware of the new organizational model, and are at least receptive to its potential for success, the customer/patient *will be* better served and given "user-friendly" service; they will ultimately feel more comfortable and trusting of their healthcare organization.

Progressive Healthcare Organizational Models

We will now discuss in significant detail the five most prominent healthcare organizational models, which are all currently in use throughout the United States and Canada; each has a specific value, benefit, and future potential for the reader's organization. We will describe also each model's inner workings, its specific nuances, its intent, and its overall ability to meet the customer/patient's escalating demands. Moreover, a diagram will be presented—in an "organizational chart" fashion—to help the reader understand each model's specific fluidity, action orientation, and interdependent dynamics.

We will also specify the potential liabilities of each organizational model. Unfortunately, like many things in our profession, one size does not fit all. The reader must thoughtfully analyze each model as it applies specifically to his or her organization. Accordingly, discussion will be provided about how best to customize, calibrate, and "tailor" for each model.

Specific steps for implementation are required for each organizational model. Each model possesses a certain style that affects its implementation, acceptance by the patient, and approval by staff members and managers. Thus, each model has a specific set of criteria that ensures its success following implementation.

The success of any healthcare organizational reconstruction rests with the competency and commitment of the individual manager and supervisor. Accordingly, methods of motivating managers to implement each of the models will also be discussed. Continuity steps and final assessment criteria will also be provided in our discussion.

Finally, individual accountabilities, responsibilities, and leadership roles for each model should be discussed. Some organizational models possess the potential to affect individual managers negatively: Power can be lost, accountabilities can be shifted, and daily action can be drastically altered in certain models. The "wrong mix" of an existing organizational model with a new one can do more harm than good. The potential for this lies in management reaction and employee response to the new model, and this will be discussed in a pragmatic, "real world" manner.

In order to garner the most value from the upcoming review of these five models, readers should:

1. consider current organizational models and their relevant shortcomings given current conditions and future demands;

2. trust their intuition and "gut instincts" about each organizational model;

3. focus on how individual managers and employees who care about the institution might "fit" into the new organizational model, rather than focusing on "nonplayer" employees who dislike any type of change or movement;

4. determine which model is most "user-friendly" to the current patient population;

5. determine which model is most "user-friendly" to the staff and workforce management;

6. consider which model would help the organization maintain the highest degree of fluidity, interdependence, and service orientation to your customer/patient community;

7. determine which model would most naturally complement any rightsizing or reconstruction effort already undertaken;

8. assess which model would be the *most* effective in the eyes of *most* of your employees and *most* of your patients;

9. consider as a secondary feature the "cosmetic appeal" of each model. Try to determine which title, model depiction, or action mechanics would be most appealing to the majority of the individuals in your organization. If such features are similar to other, more practical "baseline" considerations, you have probably picked the right model; and

10. recognize, above all, that none of these models is absolute in content or rigid in structure. Each can be customized, altered, retitled, and modified to meet any organization's specific requirements.

Keep an open mind as you review each model. Remember that none of these is the proverbial "magic bullet." Most of all, trust your business acumen, sense of leadership values, and the needs of your patient/customers to use the following five models, in their entirety or individually, as a guiding beacon for your organizational reconstruction and future renewal.

The Product-Line Model

The product-line model is designed to combine a healthcare organization's services into "product lines." The genesis of this model occurred in American industry in the 1960s, when major organizations began subdividing their corporations into various divisions. A prominent example of this can be seen in many Fortune 100 firms such as General Motors and Bristol-Myers. In both these examples, individual products—in one case cars, and in the other pharmaceutical and healthcare products—were manufactured and "vertically integrated" in each division. That is, one division—such as the Pontiac division of General Motors—would contain all of the marketing, production, human resources, and financial components necessary to make Firebirds, Trans Ams, and other Pontiac automobiles. Similarly, Bristol-Myers used its organizational structure to create "product-line divisions," which would alternatively manufacture over-the-counter pharmaceuticals, prescription pharmaceuticals, cosmetics—even hair products, though in their Clairol division (Lombardi 1984).

In recent years, the product-line model has become more popular with healthcare organizations, where it has provided a clearer definition of services for the benefit of patient and employee alike. Used primarily in recent years by large organizations, the product-line structure allows an institution to reorganize in a natural, service-generated sequence, which is this model's strong point. In a large healthcare organization, patients can sometimes become confused when looking for the services they desire. When they are unable to find them, they naturally become frustrated with—and even mistrustful of—the institution. This creates the worst sentiment possible in hospital-patient relations: the betrayal felt by a patient who cannot receive basic healthcare services.

With a product-line orientation, it becomes easier for patients to identify where they need to go to receive the services they desire. A feature of product-line implementation at some large healthcare facilities is that individual geographic locations—perhaps a specific building or a denoted wing of the hospital—become the product-line "center." By using a simple color-coded map, a patient requiring mental health outpatient services, for example, can go to the Yellow Wing, while a patient requiring neonatal services can go to the Blue Wing.

As suggested in Figure 5.2, the product-line organizational chart is easy to understand. The leadership of the product-line institution must simply determine which products will be offered and reorganize the path into these basic service areas. For example, at many larger healthcare organizations, the mental health product line incorporates the uses and abilities of clinical psychology components, social worker components, drug and alcohol rehabilitation, and other related services. By combining these services in a classic streamlining of capacities, patients not only understand *how* to access these services, but they can greater appreciate

Figure 5.2 Product-Line Model

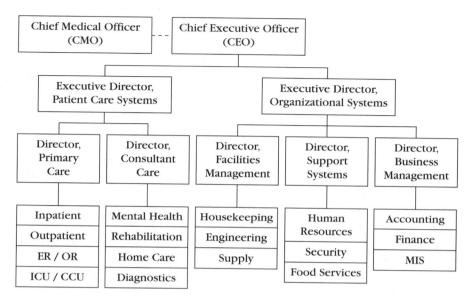

the fact that their local healthcare provider actually *possesses* the capacity to provide these services.

Another feature of the product-line organizational model is that it distinguishes front-line services from supporting services. Those services directly relevant to the patient—such as nursing, surgery, intensive care units, and other direct patient services—are collated and categorized for easy access and identification. The supporting services, such as human resources, management information services, financial services, and other administrative components, are grouped in a manner that is easily recognized by staff members. This not only creates an organizational model that is easy to understand, but it demonstrates a "patient-focused" commitment.

There are, of course, certain drawbacks to the product-line model. The first, oddly enough, is its name. Many who work in healthcare facilities are still reluctant to accept that healthcare has become largely, over the past twenty years, a business as much as a service-oriented humanistic trust. Most healthcare experts, obviously, will suggest that it is both (Smith and Kaluzny 1986). To some, however, the term "product line" represents the final, almost apocalyptic, sign of removing the human element from the healthcare organization. This sentiment must be taken into account when considering the sensitive nature of reconstruction; it can also contribute to the escalation of fear among staff members.

Furthermore, dividing organizational components into direct patient care and support services can sometimes imply to support personnel that they are "second-class organizational citizens." This perception cannot simply be ameliorated by semantics but must be addressed by using titles and other mechanics to reinforce the overall importance of each individual area. For example, as illustrated in Figure 5.2, each product line has a director—equal in importance, rank, and compensation—at its head. Therefore, the patient services sector is as important to the organization as the human resources capacity.

Perhaps an even greater risk with the product-line model is the issue of "turfs." It has been the author's experience that product-line implementation can bring about intense turf wars as individuals lose titles, staff, accountabilities, and perceived stature within the organization. Again, this might be countered by delicately assigning new titles to individual areas, as well as maintaining individual responsibilities and accountabilities, as has been discussed in the sections on rightsizing, as well as in the case study in Chapter 8.

The issue of "turf wars," however, can be easily eliminated by combining similar departments and work roles into a centralized entity. By combining various aspects of mental health services into one department, for example, duplication of individual responsibilities and other potential wastes in terms of human resources maximization can be quickly identified and addressed. For example, the author recently discovered that three mental health components, which had previously operated independently, had a combined patient capacity utilization of only 50 percent. By combining all three components into one mental health division using a product-line structure, two management jobs were eliminated—which resulted not only in an increase of productivity but the removal of two ineffectual supervisors who were described as "morale busters" by their own employees!

While such gains are not always possible when implementing product-line models, this example clearly shows one of the less obvious advantages of the product-line model: The organization will naturally become "lean and green" as each product line becomes responsible for its own profit and loss, patient service, and other quantitative measurements for success. The product-line model can be customized to include outpatient services as well as inpatient services, for example, which can then trigger the creation of criteria and standards for success in both areas. The product-line model can be adjusted over time to reflect new needs in the customer/patient community and adapted to maximize particular existing organizational strengths.

To implement the product-line model, the organization must first consider its own strengths and weaknesses relative to current patient services. Particular dimensions of the organization that are clearly profitable in terms of volume, revenue, and utilization should be given prominent consideration in the product-line reorganization, as should such valuable components as human resources and financial management, and all of their respective subcomponents.

Next, the organization should strive to identify product-line areas that they believe, based on current data and future potential, will contribute to the institution's success scheme. These areas typically include clinics, outpatient facilities, preventive medicine components, and other growing areas of healthcare organizations. It is vital to remember that emergent components of the product-line organization should be those that have already clearly proved their value to the organization, as opposed to entities that have great potential but have not produced clear, substantial contributions to the organization. Product-line areas that have great potential, but have not yet produced great revenue, can be categorized into "business development areas" and included as a subset of other product-line areas, as indicated in Figure 5.2.

Organizational leadership should then devise a product-line model that best reflects the primary areas of revenue generation, patient services, and significant institutional support. After doing so, management should be divided into vice presidents of each product-line area, supported by directors and then supervisors and managers of critical subcomponents or work teams. If possible, there should be no more than seven product lines in any healthcare organization: More than seven can dilute the organizational power and the solidity of the structure, and less than seven can limit the organization and usually result in components with no natural relationship being "forced together." For example, moving an organization to one product-line area labeled "administrative services," which includes finance and human resources, can result in a plethora of problems, not the least of which is the appointment of a vice president who might understand human resources but not have any notion of finance.

In summary, the product-line model has more advantages than disadvantages. It lets an organization consolidate its resources and reorganize in a clear, comprehensive fashion; it also affords a sense of user-friendliness to an institution's customer/patients and employees. In addition to allowing each component to act independently while still being an integrated part of a larger healthcare organization, this model is simple, clear, and flexible and can allow a manager to maintain a hands-off management approach.

The Action-Line Model

The action-line model is built on the time-honored organizational pyramid suggested by Peter Drucker and other noted management experts (Drucker 1964). However, unlike the product-line model, the action-line model is based on *function*, rather than product.

As reflected in Figure 5.3, the action-line model is centrally based with the executive staff at its core. The most effective way to depict it is to begin with the titles of the leadership and their particular functions. As illustrated in Figure 5.3, the primary executive in the action-line model is the CEO, who, in this case, has the traditional responsibilities of the president or CEO, including board and community relations and, of course, comprehensive control of the organization's overall and daily operations. A review of the six officers who report to the CEO provides an efficient perspective of the action-line model.

The first is the Chief Administration Officer (CAO), who oversees human resources and other administrative responsibilities. The CAO should be well versed in human resources, but must also have the management dexterity to deal with food services and security, among other divisional aspects. The Chief Financial Officer oversees the institution's financial and accounting responsibilities. The duties of the Chief Operating Officer are traditional to most healthcare organizations and are usually called "operational responsibilities." The Chief Nursing Officer is responsible for nursing and patient services, and the Chief Medical Officer, as the lead physician in the organization, provides a strong

Figure 5.3 Action-Line Model

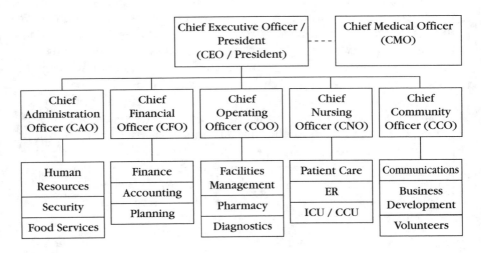

link to physician relations and medical services. This individual merits compensation based on the commitment, support, and performance of the medical staff.

The most unique officer in the action-line model is the Chief Community Officer (CCO), who is responsible for public relations, organizational communication, community relations, business development, and other duties. Like the Chief Medical Officer, the CCO is a position that is often overlooked, if not nonexistent, in a typical healthcare organization. However, in many ways, the CCO is not only as important as the other chief officers, but, in a sense, is even more important as healthcare becomes more of a community trust.

There are many advantages to the action-line model. First, by streamlining the reporting relationship to the CEO into these six components, the entire organization is given a distinct hierarchical orientation. This is particularly helpful in smaller healthcare organizations, which is why this model may be ideal for smaller community hospitals and similar nonprofit healthcare organizations. Second, the organizational hierarchy becomes more fluid in the action-line model. Vice president positions are either completely eliminated or assigned to chief officers who have seniority *and* high level of performance. Directors report to the chief officers, and managers report to the directors, giving the organization four tiers of management, which allows for vertical career paths for promotion and career advancement.

A third advantage of the action-line model is that it allows the organization to recommit itself to the community and its physicians. In many organizations, a major lament on the part of patients is that the organization has "lost touch with the community" or that "the physicians operate as separate entities." In the action-line model, the ability to employ physicians, have a senior executive in touch with the community, and to make sure that the two essential dimensions of community and physicians are given top priority is accomplished in a clear, distinct manner. In essence, the overall objective of the action-line model is to highlight physician contribution, community awareness, and comprehensive provision of healthcare services.

A fourth advantage of the action-line model is its clarity. As it is not a radical departure from the more traditional model of a healthcare organization, the transformation to the action-line model will be neither dramatic nor unnecessarily startling to employees or patients. Provided that the organization stresses the move to an action-line model as a commitment to physician involvement, community service, and efficiency of action, most organizational stakeholders will accept change. If these three goals are not clearly communicated, however, community and staff alike will question the move.

The only drawback—and it can be a major one—is the simplicity of the model. Staff might wonder why the organization "rightsized" to get to an action-line model. However, as we have discussed repeatedly throughout this book, if the rightsizing is done prior to the introduction of the action-line model, this one drawback can be easily overcome, as the model implementation is more fluid and exact because of the "right size" of organizational members.

To implement the action-line model, the CEO should first determine if internal candidates exist who can fill the responsibilities of all six of the chief officer positions. Second, if there are no internal candidates, outside candidates should be hired at the time of the transition. This gives the CEO the opportunity to revamp the executive staff as well as to eliminate unqualified individuals from senior executive positions. Next, the CEO should combine all departments into the six general areas of the action-line model. Again, this lets the CEO streamline the organization logically to focus on providing optimal patient service.

Subsequent to the appointment of all six chief officers, management-by-objective (MBO) performance evaluation systems should be implemented. Each chief officer's goals and objectives should reflect the needs and objectives of their entire scope of responsibility. The goals should be as well defined as possible and incorporate the needs of the organization, their specific divisions, and individual leadership goals.

The Decentralized-Decision Model

The decentralized-decision model is best used at an organization that is composed of various components with different responsibilities. For example, as indicated in Figure 5.4, an organization that is geographically diverse or made up of different components is a likely candidate for the decentralized-decision model. This model uses the individual talents and expertise of all organizational members by employing a basic organizational structure that is the same for each component but still allows a great degree of flexibility for individual action and leadership.

The decentralized-decision model is premised on the mission of each individual component. This mission—in terms of the services the component provides and its own unique patient focus—dictates the daily operations of the suborganization. Assume for example that a mental health organization is structured as a decentralized-decision model. This institution has an outpatient clinic, which has a different mission than the organization's inpatient facility. Though these missions may be different,

Figure 5.4 The Decentralized-Decision Model

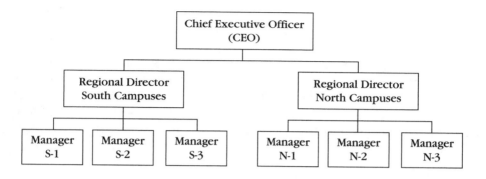

however, the basic organizational structure of each suborganization is the same, and both use two aspects of strength.

The first aspect of strength is leadership. Each component has a titular leader, who must be a skilled manager and technically expert in his or her area. The individual director is responsible for the actions, development, and performance of the managers, who must also be both technically expert and managerially proficient. These are prerequisites for success in the decentralized-decision model for two basic reasons: First, each component of this model must provide a certain service to the community and act as an independent entity within the organization. If the leadership of any component is technically expert but not knowledgeable about financial or management concerns, service will suffer. Second—and conversely—if the director of a subcomponent in a decentralized-decision model organization is a good manager but not technically expert, quality of service can erode, illnesses can be misdiagnosed, and other such technical problems can occur.

The second strength of the decentralized-decision model is that each subcomponent becomes an independent entity, contributing to the common good of the organization. This allows the directors to exert their own special brand of influence, apply their individual expertise, and grow and develop as leaders as they maintain accountability and responsibility. The decentralized-decision model, therefore, allows a sense of autonomy at each subcomponent, which in turn encourages employees to act accountably and as independent agents with interdependent responsibilities to their colleagues, and in a larger sense, to other organizational entities.

However, this is also this model's greatest risk. Certain entities can become "runaway engines" if a director becomes too autonomous or the subcomponent begins to believe that it is more important—or less important—than any other subcomponent. Naturally, this mandates the need for strong leadership at every level of the decentralized organization.

Communication is essential to the success of a decentralized organization, as leaders must know the overall goals of their organization and must translate those into specific objectives for their subcomponent. Strategic planning and team evaluation are vital components in the management scheme of a decentralized-decision organizational model.

The advantages of a decentralized-decision model organization are its autonomy, reliance on technical expertise, and the ability of each leader to act quickly and positively without a rigid, overriding, organizational structure. If the CEO of the decentralized organization makes certain to:

- communicate effectively, efficiently, and daily;
- guard against the placing of "maverick" managers at any level of the decentralized organization;
- fully understand the individual capacities, components, and strengths and weaknesses of each subcomponent; and
- ensure the contribution of each decentralized component to the overall organizational scheme,

this model can work extremely effectively.

In fact, by maintaining these four standards as daily leadership objectives, the CEO will soon discover that this model affords the organization the greatest amount of management development, individual growth, and customer/patient service conceivable for an organization that may be regionally diverse and varying in expertise. Furthermore, this model allows for growth, development, and expansion, based on increasing customer/patient need.

The Triad Model

The triad model originated in many federal healthcare institutions but has recently been redefined to become an extremely effective model used in a wide assortment of other healthcare organizations. In both large and small facilities, the triad model can be extremely effective, as it is simple, clear, and commited to the patient—all essential ingredients in any organizational model.

As depicted in Figure 5.5, the triad model consists of a CEO and three reporting executives. The first is the Chief Medical Officer, who is responsible for the entire medical service provision of the organization, which includes nursing, patient services, and diagnostic services.

The second reporting executive is the Chief Business Officer, who, as the title indicates, oversees the business responsibilities of the organization. This includes accounting and finance, in addition to other

Figure 5.5   The Triad Model

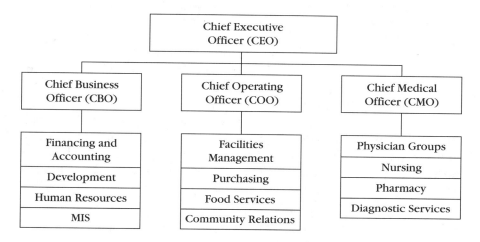

considerations such as community development, human resources management, and other essential commercial responsibilities. As healthcare organizations become as focused on business aspects as they are on patient service aspects, the Chief Business Officer becomes an essential focal point in both the transformation process as well as the continuity of organizational development.

The third member of the reporting triad is the Chief Operations Officer, who is responsibile for the operational facets, including supplies, transport, maintenance, and housekeeping.

This triad can be modified to combine the responsibilities of the Chief Business Officer with those of the Chief Operations Officer, resulting in a triad of the Chief Executive Officer, the Chief Medical Officer, and the Chief Operations Officer. This is only one modification that can be made to this model. As suggested by the diagram, certain other aspects of the organization, such as the legal capacity, can report directly to the CEO; additionally, the community relations function can also report directly to the CEO to achieve the emphasis delineated in the action-line model. The triad model can be used in large organizations—and in fact has for years in many Veterans Administration facilities across the country—or in a smaller organization with equal success. In a real sense, the triad organization represents the ultimate streamlining of a healthcare organization, as lines of report are reduced to three basic areas, all of which report to the Chief Executive Officer.

As suggested by the diagram, however, the triad model must have three reporting areas in order to be effective, which is both the model's strength and weakness. Vertical promotional opportunities and career advancement can be limited in the triad, as the top of the "pyramid" is narrower than in other organizational models. However, lines of report are extremely clear in the triad model, and career development facets are clearly defined from the outset of the introduction of the model.

Implementing this model is extremely easy. Fundamentally, financially distressed organizations are perfect candidates for the triad model, as management positions can be eliminated quickly and effectively as it is introduced. While this will obviously produce some negative repercussions, it will also reduce the amount of management layers within the organization—which in many healthcare organizations could help solve some problems. A major requirement of the triad model is the rank structure of management, which should be as follows:

1. **Executives,** defined as individuals who have profit/loss responsibility, with major segments of personnel as part of their management responsibilities.
2. **Directors,** who are individuals who have financial and human resources responsibilities to manage.
3. **Managers,** who have personnel management responsibilities.
4. **Specialists,** who have either financial or technical duties, but not personnel management responsibilities.

This hierarchy eliminates the confusion that exists in many healthcare organizations that have too many layers of management. The triad model can clearly define management levels, responsibilities, and individual accountabilities, which in return will strengthen the overall organization.

The Traditional Organizational Model

The model illustrated in Figure 5.6 will be immediately recognized by many readers who have worked in traditional community hospitals and other healthcare entities. This traditional model uses a CEO, who maintains as a direct report a Chief Operating Officer, who in turns oversees an assortment of other vice presidents. This model can best be used in organizations with five hundred employees or more; in smaller institutions it can be overly grandiose and ineffective.

The strength of the traditional model is its ability to allow the CEO to act as a conduit to the patient community, board of directors, and other essential stakeholders, while the Chief Operating Officer controls the internal operations of the healthcare facility. This is a traditional model throughout American industry and, in fact, is widely believed to have found its origin in the structure of military organizations (Langguth 1988).

Figure 5.6 The Traditional Organizational Model

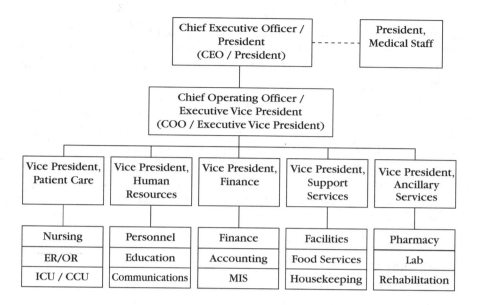

The traditional organizational model affords many benefits. Lines of report are clear, the organization is structured based on action and technical responsibilities, and the opportunity for promotion and advancement is apparent. Further, emphasis on each particular component is reflected in the organizational chart. In traditional organizational models, the management hierarchy can consist of vice presidents, directors, managers, and supervisors, which again clearly delineates to employees and patients *who* holds the power.

The traditional model can certainly be applied to a community hospital. The one caveat that should be made is that external responsibilities—as the domain of the CEO—and internal responsibilities—as the domain of the Chief Operating Officer—must be kept separate. This distinction has not been made often enough, in the author's estimation, at many community hospitals. When these two lines become blurred, individuals working at the organization can question "who's in charge," and decisions can be made haphazardly or in an overlapping, nonproductive fashion.

The traditional model should not be lightly discounted. In times of change, simplicity, clarity, and stability are highly valued by the typical healthcare employee. Accordingly, this model should be considered as closely and as stridently as the other four models described throughout this chapter.

When considering the traditional model, creativity must be applied when considering outpatient services, outlying health facilities, business development, strategic planning, and other emerging facets that are part of the modern healthcare organization. The traditional model can be restrictive in embracing these facets, or misguide the customer/patient and employee if not properly collated and incorporated in this particular organizational model.

Each organizational model has its own features, strengths, and weaknesses. By using the selection criteria specified at the beginning of this chapter and, moreover, by using the organizational model as the centerpiece of the reconstruction process, the reader can make an enlightened decision that will increase organizational allegiance, capitalize on the rightsizing effort, bring closure to the restructuring process, and begin the all-important renewal process. The organizational model, in summary, is part of the overall reorganization process—*not* the reason for transformation.

References

Drucker, P. F. 1964. *Managing for Results*. New York: Harper & Row.

Langguth, A. J. 1988. *Patriots*. New York: Touchstone.

Lombardi, D. N. 1984. *Psycho-Communicative Dynamics of Industry*. St. Louis, MO: University Press.

———. 1993. *Progressive Healthcare Management Strategies*. Chicago: American Hospital Publishing.

———. 1996. *Thriving in an Age of Change*. Chicago: Health Administration Press.

Smith, D. B., and A. D. Kaluzny. 1986. *The White Labyrinth*. Chicago: Health Administration Press.

LEADING THE RENEWAL PROCESS

P erhaps the most pivotal part of the entire transformation process is organizational renewal. During this phase, the healthcare institution must address its present challenges and ensure its future progress by recommitting its human resources, medical and technical strengths, and combined organizational power toward addressing the needs and desires of the patient community.

In a sense, organizational renewal is the most overlooked aspect of transformation. Many healthcare leaders focus on a new organizational model or on the rightsizing effort without considering the organizational renewal. This is unfortunate: Renewal possesses the greatest potential for failure of the reorganization process, primarily because renewal encompasses the commitment of all staff members toward the model and helps to build on the benefits of rightsizing and reorganization.

Briefly, organizational renewal is the process in which an institution rededicates itself as a reformed organization—built upon past successes and traditions—that has remodeled to meet future demands. In this chapter, we will discuss the basic objectives of organizational renewal, the approaches necessary to overcome individual resistance to it, the leadership roles and strategies that must be used, and the essential leadership dynamics. By incorporating the practical strategies discussed here—and by avoiding some of the potential pitfalls to be specified— readers can establish a practical strategy to renew their organizations successfully.

The Objectives of Organizational Renewal

Recommitting to Customer/Patients

The renewal process is the final phase of organizational transformation, which has ten objectives; the first is to demonstrate a recommitment to the patient. By undertaking an entire reorganization process—that is, rightsizing the institution, reconstructing it with a new organizational model, and positioning itself toward greater customer/patient service— the healthcare organization has demonstrated a commitment to the customer/patient's present and future healthcare needs. If the renewal process is successful, every staff member will see it as the starting point for a long-term organizational strategy that will provide better care and more services with greater efficiency.

Implementing the Organizational Model

The second objective of renewal is to launch the new organizational model, which can create greater flexibility for the healthcare organization, an increased ability to address future healthcare concerns, and the dexterity to grow in pace with the customer/patient community. The renewal process, in effect, should help to launch the new model into the sphere of practicality and everyday use.

Validating the Rightsizing

The renewal process must validate any rightsizing effort that might have taken place in the organization. Perhaps the biggest threat to morale is feeling that any rightsizing action had no discernible benefit to the employee or the customer/patient. The renewal process should reinforce that the rightsizing was a good long-term strategy. The best way to do this is for management to highlight the benefits of the reconstruction process and stress that without the rightsizing effort, none of them would have been possible.

Meeting Future Demands

Renewal must help the institution meet future demands, especially by providing a "new way of doing things." Past the theoretic aspects of a new organizational model and the negative ramifications of rightsizing, renewal is the organization's first attempt to address old problems in a new manner. Most healthcare professionals will agree that doing so is necessary, given the constant changes in the environment.

Implementing New Processes

Renewal offers an excellent starting point to implement new processes. A major failing in the renewal process occurs when an organization does not enact new processes and strategies in a timely fashion. This is most apparent when an institution introduces a new organizational model and then spends an inordinate amount of time discussing it, reflecting on its potential value, and debating its aesthetic nature—and not immediately charging every staff member to "try it out" in their daily responsibilities. Every staff member must be given the opportunity to experiment with the new model, implement new processes, and in a real sense, try to find a "better way" of doing things in the reformed organization.

Empowering the Employee

The renewed organization must place the individual employee at the focal point for implementing change. The renewal process has to stress the accountability and responsibility of each organizational member for its success and, ultimately, for its ability to afford greater healthcare service to the customer/patient. A mistake commonly made by executives is to assume too much responsibility for the success of the renewal. As a result, any failures are perceived as the executive's fault. In a progressive healthcare organization, all of the members of the organization share the credit—as well as the blame, if any–during the transformation.

Activating Leadership

In a "leaner and greener" healthcare organization, leaders—throughout every level of the institution—determine the action and success of the healthcare organization; naturally they will assume a greater amount of responsibility for motivating their staff. The renewal process should give these leaders direction for undertaking their daily leadership responsibilities.

Using the Past

The healthcare organization's past tradition and legacy offer a valuable building block for its future. It is vital that leaders not discount *everything* from the past when introducing and implementing a new organizational model. Renewal, to be most effective, should balance past tradition with future direction.

Planning for the Future

As North American society changes from a manufacturing-industrial society to a service-oriented one, different expectations and needs will arise in the customer/patient community. Viewing this through the prism of reorganization and transformation, the modern healthcare institution must adopt a new vision for success, replete with a new credo, new organizational systems, and effective leadership. This new vision must be articulate, comprehensive, and relevant for the majority of employees and all members of the customer/patient community.

Introducing Better Systems

Finally, organizational renewal must introduce better organizational systems. Organizational renewal is the perfect opportunity to implement new systems to better serve the patient and to encourage greater performance from every staff member. This opportunity to introduce better organizational systems is not only a good side-effect of organizational transformation, but in many cases can ensure the long-term success of that transformation.

By first understanding the objectives of organizational renewal, and then embracing the leadership strategies, roles, and imperatives necessary to implement them, the healthcare executive can ensure a successful, smooth organizational transformation.

Leadership Imperatives

There are three fundamental leadership imperatives during the renewal process that ensure a successful organizational transformation. First, leaders must encourage a sense of interdependence among all of their reporting sections and personnel. Second, a sense of unity must be enhanced by the leader as the organization undergoes change. Finally the leader must reinforce the credibility of the organization and its leadership.

In the following sections, we will analyze these leadership imperatives and then specifically delineate five subcomponents of each. In addition to defining and explaining their importance, strategies to implement each imperative will also be provided.

Interdependence

A sense of interdependence must be installed in the transformed organization as quickly as possible. The old adage that "Nobody wins unless we all win," perhaps best typifies interdependence. In the past, a patient might be likely, for example, to believe that the hospital was generally a good healthcare provider, with only a few substandard departments. The patient would be forgiving of the shortcomings of the organization if, overall, good service was provided.

Now, however, patients are not as forgiving and in fact tend to view the entire organization as a single entity. Believing that they are well educated by the media and other sources, patients are very circumspect about their care. The author was recently told by a director of food service that "Everybody nowadays is an expert on food, and particularly chicken salad!" An hour later, the director of radiology at the same hospital said, "Nowadays, everyone thinks they are an expert on radiology—and particularly MRI!" Put bluntly, everybody nowadays believes that they are an expert on everything in healthcare! To use another worn cliché, "The chain is only as strong as its weakest link." With these anecdotes—and this cliché—in mind, it is vital to understand not only the importance of interdependence but its five main components and how they can create an interdependent workplace.

Clarity

The first interdependence dynamic is that of *clarity*, which can be defined as a clear delineation of the organization's mission, values, and future goals in an easily understood manner. Additionally, clarity should be supplemented by ensuring that staff members understand the relationship between job scope and organizational goals. That is, they should not only clearly understand their new job responsibility but how those new duties fit into the new organization. This is the responsibility of both the leader and the employee, at each departmental level, as well as the organization's executive leadership.

Clarity can be achieved in a number of ways. Publishing and posting mission statements can increase understanding of the new organization's intent, objectives, and overall mission. The institution should also clarify work roles, perhaps by using the job analysis techniques described earlier. Further, the organization should also publicize success criteria for the entire organization, as well as for each new department or team. Each manager should define the success criteria for every individual who reports to him or her.

As the new organization takes shape and enters its initial stage of daily action, goals should be discussed and any learning that is accomplished by any staff members should be shared in the interests of educating all employees. Each departmental manager should also discuss the organizaton's community reputation and current direction and their impact on present and future goals relative to the specific department. The goals and objectives of the new organization should also be given to all employees. This can be done with a CEO report, for example.

Clarity can also be achieved by constant reinforcement of mission organizational values by supervisors in daily activities and regular meetings.

Beyond simply stressing organizational values, leaders should seek to link daily action, individual successes, and departmental achievements to organizational values and mission objectives. The timely explanation of new organizational directives and changing goals by management to all members of the organization is also key to clarity. This helps to negate rumors and other negative communication, which we have discussed in other semblances throughout this text. The intelligent use of organizational communication devices, such as newsletters and employee forums, should be used to present organizational directions and new dynamics. Additionally, focused presentations regarding change dynamics and new organizational directives, supplemented with dialogue-based communication in those presentations, is also useful in achieving clarity (see Chapter 8).

Additionally, leaders at every level should be aware of certain less-apparent methods in which they could promote clarity in the transformed organization. For example, when interviewing job candidates for open positions, the new organization's values and mission should be discussed with the candidate and embellished in the orientation process for new organizational members. Publication and establishment of organizational goals, values, and current objectives by senior managers must be augmented and discussed relative to specific departmental application by all organizational leaders. Moreover, the manager at every level should never take an "ostrich approach" to change dynamics in the transformed organization. Questions should be answered promptly and in cases where the manager does not have an answer relative to new organizational initiative, the answer should be sought and delivered to employees immediately. As always, communication is the key to action and success in the reorganization process, and this is as apparent in the renewal process as it is in the rightsizing and reconstruction stages of transformation.

Contribution

The second interdependence dynamic is that of *contribution*, which is the individual staff member's participation in accomplishing work objectives, as well as independent action generated consistently that enhances the organization. The transformed organization will only be as strong as each individual member, and it is the leader's responsibility to ensure that all staff members contribute immediately and optimally.

This is accomplished by setting clear, measurable work goals. Contribution is shown by selfless dedication to these goals and imperatives and by self-motivated individual work action that is of constant high quality. Accordingly, it is the responsibility of the leader to set individual goals to ensure maximum individual contribution to the ultimate departmental and organizational success.

Because self-directed improvement defines the "superstar" contributor in the renewed institution, healthcare leaders should constantly encourage all staff members to devise "better ways of doing things," particularly if these new ways can be attributed to the new organizational structure. The leader should not dictate goals without active participation by individual members and the entire work group. To do this, the healthcare leader must communicate with his or her staff not only *ASAP* but *AMAP*—that is, As Soon As Possible and As Much As Possible. Open communication when setting departmental goals leads not only to a sense of trust but to one of interdependence, which has a direct bearing on how well and how often an employee will contribute to the organization.

Contribution is enhanced by leadership styles that are open yet directed, flexible but not flaccid, and encouraging but not coddling. Most of all, leaders must encourage all staff members to take responsibility for providing not only performance, but sound input, timely suggestions, and solid action.

Mutuality

The third interdependence imperative is that of *mutuality*, best defined as a firm commitment to the common goals and objectives of the organization, as well as a clear understanding of the need to share information, viewpoints, and critical expertise. Mutuality is apparent in a department in which work is provided by the overwhelming majority of employees that supports the organization's commitment to the customer/patient. Conducting sessions in which vital information is discussed and related to objectives also builds a sense of mutuality, as do regular debriefing sessions in which the significant actions and critical contributions of staff are reviewed.

Mutuality is also fostered by effective mentoring and cross-training programs for both new staff members as well as existing ones who may lack specific technical knowledge. Effective orientation programs should not only help the new employee understand the goals and mission of the organization, but also the organization's specific operating procedures. Performance reviews and other assessment methods that clearly reward accomplishments also add to the mutuality of an institution.

There are five factors that can destroy mutuality in the renewed organization:

1. the traits of self-interest, self-aggrandizement, and self-promotion being encouraged by organizational action and performance reward systems;

2. the proliferation of work environments in which communication and perceptive learning are discouraged by environmental restraints or leadership ignorance. Conducting regular meetings and communicating as much as possible can counter this particular problem;

3. the existence of a rigid organizational structure in which communication barriers and a lack of focus are not only obvious but enforced by management. Mutuality cannot exist in an environment where individuals feel they cannot speak;

4. a lack of common objectives, mission, value standards, and central organizational goals. The obvious countermeasure is to disseminate the institution's goals, missions, and values whenever and however possible; and

5. limited managerial efforts to stress cooperation and coordination among divisions. Organizational leadership should address this by eliminating self-absorbed managers in the rightsizing process, setting goals that reflect institutional adherence to team standards and similar "barrier breaker" initiatives, and using a new organizational model that will help destroy self-contained "turfs" and "fiefdoms."

Mutuality is based on optimum use of resources, common goals, confidence and trust in each organizational entity and fellow staff member, and a sense of pride throughout the organization. In the renewed organization, these are all requisites for success.

Openness

The fourth interdependence factor is that of *openness*. A sense of openness is evident in an organization where communication is honest and direct, and each staff member is encouraged to assess action plans and regularly present opinions, information, and suggestions. This does not mean that individuals are allowed to define problems without solutions, complain unnecessarily, or simply lament the demise of the old organizational structure—or any other "nonplayer" communication. Nonplayers are well known for such negative strategies. See the appendix for other such tactics and the ways to counter them effectively.

An organization that embraces openness as an interdependence dynamic encourages and rewards employees whose contributory "first guesses" and other innovations result in positive performance. Past the implementation of a simple suggestion box, the renewed organization should make every attempt to reward innovations and successes that are achieved under the auspices of the renewed organizational structure.

Exemplary listening skills also contribute to openness. Encouraging managers and supervisors to ask incisive questions will elicit good answers from employees. Good listening can also reinforce employee trust of management and organizational leadership as a whole. A sense of openness can lead to increased knowledge for all members of the organization, and particularly for leaders at every level.

Positivity

The final dynamic of the interdependence imperative is that of *positivity*. Past clichés, positivity is reflected by a group and organizational allegiance to progressive action, as shown by work discussions, operational plans, and overall dedication to the customer/patient. Positivity is often a product of the first four interdependence dynamics.

Leaders can engender positivity among their staff very simply: By adopting an optimistic outlook on future plans, by communicating openly and realistically, and by *acting* positive, staff members will respond accordingly. Presenting plans and offering solutions, instead of redefining old problems and dilemmas, is an essential component of positivity. The encouragement and motivation shown by managers and supervisors for new ideas and innovations naturally helps positivity, which then contributes to the entire imperative of interdependence. In a similar vein, discouragement and negative reinforcement given by managers to "nonplayers"—to include poor performance reviews, probation, and other means of discipline—will also build a sense of positivity in the renewed organization. "Nonplayers" will often present these five actions, which must be dealt with to achieve positivity among the rest of the staff:

1. encouraging or maintaining a poor attitude, as well complaining and stressing the "negative" side of anything;
2. presenting problems without solutions, questions without answers, and challenges without progressive action;
3. acting like "martyrs and victims" in work discussions, particularly by those who feel victimized by organizational transformation;
4. putting their own selfish interests ahead of those of the customer/patient; and
5. failing to implement positive suggestions and ideas quickly and demonstrably throughout the organization.

The first four of these dilemmas have been discussed in this text and will be further detailed later. Special attention must be made to the *last* detracting action, however, which should be reversed into a positive semblance. That is, any suggestions that are useful, realistic, and viable should be acted on immediately.

Interdependence is vital to the success of the renewed organization, which should not contain factions but rather a common allegiance to organizational action among all staff members.

Establishing Unity

In the renewed organization, a sense of unity must be enhanced in which all members of the organization feel as though they truly belong, as if they are part of a community. There are five ways to establish and promote unity, and all must be considered by any institution renewing itself.

Community

Community in the renewed organization is when all members feel a general sense of trust and common interests in the new organization, a sense of which is reflected in the continuing relationships with the surrounding customer/patient community (see Figure 6.1). Many employees are local residents, and usually patients, of the institution in which they work. The renewed organization must therefore demonstrate a genuine interest in the professional development and overall well-being of not only patients but employees. This can be established with such events as organizational

Figure 6.1 Healthcare Organization as a Community Vortex

picnics, special educational events, and luncheons when new organizational initiatives are unveiled.

Conscious efforts by management to engage the support and participation of all staff when making decisions that will affect the outlying community can foster a sense of belonging, of organizational unity. Similarly, perspectives from each employee, who is in contact with patients as well as neighbors and friends from the outlying locale, become vital to the launch of the renewed organization. Formal data-gathering in the community—using surveys, visitor cards, InfoCards, and other means—should also be implemented in the initial stages of organizational renewal, and using the assistance of staff members can ensure that this essential process succeeds.

Communication between major factions in the organization—principally between large employee groups and senior management—can also lead to increased unity: The possible presence of certain factions that perceive themselves as better or more important than other groups must be countered immediately. This is the primary responsibility of the individual department leader, with the support of senior management, and can be accomplished by flow charts, "show and tell" sessions between departments, or, as we have discussed, by implementing interdependence initiatives. Similarly, the organization itself must not consider itself too important or that it "knows everything" about staff and the customer/patient community. Not only is this view arrogant, but it also inhibits data gathering. Remember, during the renewal process, an organization can never know too much about a community.

Continuity

The second aspect of establishing unity is *continuity*, defined as consistent organizational progress. Continuity is particularly important during the renewal process when many employees and patients are naturally skeptical about the promised efficiency and effectiveness of the renewed organization. Ensuring that these guidelines are followed can help achieve continuity during the renewal process:

1. clear identification and timely internal publication of organizational imperatives, ideals, and current accomplishments in the renewed organization;
2. positive reaction to change consistent with the organization's overall mission and stated objectives;
3. actions and statements on behalf of management that emphasize organizational missions and goals, including proactive communication in crisis situations;

4. installation and maintenance of human resources programs that set as their goals low turnover, long tenure, and constant development of professional skills;

5. maximum coordination and cooperation between departments and new organizational entities;

6. continuous communication in times of change and crisis, presented appropriately to staff and, if necessary, to community members;

7. proper maintenance systems for management and employee turnover, such as standard operating practice systems and turnover files;

8. comprehensive understanding of managers and employees of the new policies, procedures and strategies of the renewed organization, and moreover, their relevance to individual action;

9. consistency in leadership at all levels, including new managers, new supervisors, and new employees, facilitated by their understanding of strategies, methods, and institutional goals; and

10. encouragement for the mission, values and specific organizational strategies for customer/patient service in the renewed organization. This factor is extremely important, as it is a major constant in light of all the "variables" presented by the organizational transformation.

Following these rules can maintain a sense of continuity. A basic theme through these rules is that the emphasis should be placed on the renewed organization, as opposed to the old structure. Continuity is a difficult proposition, as it seeks to combine the positive facets of the old organization with the promising efficiencies of the new one.

Interaction

Unity is also established by *interaction*, which is the participation and cooperation by all staff members in a central work activity. Interaction is also reflected in the communication between team members when working toward a specific goal. Interaction is achieved when the organization emphasizes group participation and achievement and supports individual contribution and talent. Activities to encourage informal meetings among staff can contribute to professional interaction. This can also be achieved, for example, in an action-line organization, which immediately employs the use of "action-line summits." These are simple meetings in which new members of an action-line team meet their new colleagues. Work activities that help establish a productive, professional relationship between related work units and counterpart individuals can also lead to increased interaction, which contributes to unity.

Progressive management relationships among departmental leaders that promote teamwork help to enhance unity. Timely encouragement, monitoring, and assessment of interpersonal skills, team orientation, and individual commitment—not only in the annual performance evaluation but every day—also generate solid employee interaction.

Certain management actions must be avoided at all costs. A statement by a unit manager, for instance, that his or her group is the "hub" of the hospital—or some other elitist designation—can lead to bitterness, acrimony, antipathy, and animosity among other work units. Further, if management does not reward staff contributions, then individuals can become self-absorbed and uninterested, which greatly decreases interaction. Finally, the lack of innovation, imagination, and intelligence on the part of any manager or executive when designing and promoting new group work approaches in the renewed organization sends a clear signal to the individual staff member that interaction, unity, and interdependence are merely "buzzwords"—not the cornerstones of the renewed organization.

This deficiency is not limited to managers. Staff can also cripple a sense of interaction, especially when they adopt an "I'll do my job, you do yours!" stance at the expense of steady group participation. This naturally hurts group unity and must be countered by managers as soon as possible.

Pride

Pride, the fourth factor to consider when trying to establish institutional unity, is the realistic, tangible feeling of allegiance and support for the organization. Pride can be instilled by management by highlighting the organization's past positive record of competent healthcare services, which are now being augmented by a new organizational structure.

Finally, consistent value-driven management is absolutely essential to instill pride in employees. This means that poor performance by any group or individual within the organization cannot be rewarded or condoned. Positive reaction to change in crisis within the institution and the patient community is also essential. Employees can also feel a renewed sense of pride when they identify with new organizational goals, directives, and directions. Clearly communicating organizational progress and openly embracing the basic renewed organizational values of decency, fortitude, industry, integrity, and knowledge are both foundation blocks of institutional pride.

Respect

The final way to establish unity is to build *respect*. Respect is defined here as a sense of esteem for all staff members and an appreciation for their contributions.

There are ten ways to build and reinforce organizational respect:

1. strong leadership that encourages workplace diversity and ensures that individual dignity is always maintained;
2. programs on cultural and professional diversity, the elements of team building and group achievement, and conflict resolution;
3. mission statements and credos that clearly cite respect and dignity as mandatory conditions for continued employment;
4. management action to instill a sense of pride and trust;
5. effective employee relations programs that address, assess, and resolve employee concerns and complaints;
6. the elimination of stereotypes or labels;
7. "zero tolerance" for the negative, demeaning, or discriminatory actions of managers and employees alike;
8. discipline and, if possible, dismissal of any recalcitrant, subversive, or openly disloyal manager. The best tactic in this case is to ask for the individual's resignation. If it is not given, this individual's behavior and actions should be documented with the sole purpose of eventual termination;
9. immediate resolution of any instance where the dignity of one or more employees was disrespected; and
10. the constant reinforcement throughout an employee's tenure—from hiring through education and performance evaluation—of respect and pride.

Establishing unity among staff and managers is essential to the renewed organization, where division can quickly undermine the entire renewal process. By adopting the leadership strategies discussed here, and by incorporating them as part of the new organization's daily governance, this important leadership imperative can become the way of life in the new healthcare institution.

Reinforcing Credibility

Employees and management must believe in the renewed organization and its mission and goals. This credibility must be based on the institution's ability and expertise in meeting the needs of customer/patient, as well as its internal progress and growth. That is, employees will not support an institution that they perceive as not only unable to provide the best healthcare possible but unable to take care of its business interests and staff. There are five ways to establish credibility in the minds of staff and management.

Acumen

The first way to reinforce an organization's *acumen* is to stress its commitment to employees by constantly developing staff's job-related knowledge and technical expertise. Acumen can be established through regularly scheduled events that educate employees on new techniques and skills and how they apply to the organization. Conducting the needs-analysis exercise and other similar surveys can determine specific training, educational, and developmental needs. Staff members can assist in this process by enumerating their educational and instructional needs, including cross-training. Education is extremely valued by healthcare employees, and, as a result, staff will see the institution's attempt to provide greater opportunities for that education as a benefit.

Confidence

Confidence, the second method of credibility reinforcement, is the sense felt by staff members that they are capable and ready to meet the challenges posed by the healthcare organization's primary mission—providing the best service to the institution's customer/patients. Providing *real* positive reinforcement, not lukewarm support or vacuous cheerleading, to staff members can build confidence, as can highlighting examples of exemplary performance. This can be accomplished in group meetings and other events, as we have discussed, where recent institutional successes are emphasized and celebrated.

Remember, however, when congratulating an individual to use his or her superior performance as an example of what anyone on the staff can achieve. Management must inspire confidence among staff and reward the exemplary individual but not cause resentment or jealousy, especially among those who feel they are not being similarly recognized.

Organizational credibility can be jeopardized if five actions are allowed to take place:

1. publicly castigating a well-meaning employee for poor performance;
2. constantly and disproportionately focusing on the poor organizational performance or "losses";
3. allowing a lack of educational programs, mentoring, orientation, and other development strategies that increase awareness and knowledge;
4. canceling professional programs or educational or technical training (This not only threatens an organization's credibility, it

can endanger an institution's entire renewal: Highly educated staff are a critical component of the renewal process); and

5. allowing insecure, arrogant, self-centered behavior or other character flaws—real or imagined—to linger or prosper.

Being aware of these problems is half of the solution. To solve them, management must make committing these actions as grave as, say, mismanaging an intravenous unit or mishandling a patient's medical records. Without addressing these problems this seriously, staff confidence will falter.

Investment

Investment, the next factor, is reflected by a sound managerial commitment to staff development, new programs and services, and other such initiatives. Ample financial support for salaries and benefits, employee education, and human resources programs also helps reinforce the institution's investment in employee development. Similarly, rewarding long-term performance and laudable contributions, as well as encouraging and empowering employees to take an ardent interest in their organization as more than just an employer or a place to collect a paycheck, all reflect the organization's sense of investment.

Progress

Progress is the fourth component of credibility reinforcement. The renewed healthcare organization must demonstrate growth and development as measured by a greater collective talent base, more capable staff, and improved ability to render services to the customer/patient community. By visibly highlighting the attainment of all goals—large or small—special departmental performance, and outstanding individual contributions, staff can see that the institution is making the transition to a new organizational model smoothly and successfully. When necessary, recalibrating, redirecting, and resetting organizational goals can let employees know that the institution is making every realistic effort to meet them. Insisting on trust, pride, professionalism, and responsibility from all members of the organization at all times is necessary to ensure progress.

Versatility

The staff's collective expertise, acquired knowledge, and practical perspectives that allow the institution to manage a wide variety of situations successfully and meet all new challenges defines an organization's *versatility*. Using this collective knowledge, and acquiring new talent to bolster an organization's technical and professional abilities, reinforces an organization's credibility among staff.

Effective staff recruitment and ongoing personnel development also increase an institution's versatility. Conversely, limited opportunities for internal growth and professional development can quickly destroy morale and credibility, as can restricted contact with other departments and work units that might increase professional expertise. Management must be alert to this, and should also avoid restrictive job descriptions or a narrow professional focus or range of daily activities. One way to accomplish this is to let employees participate in job development strategies, contribute to their own job description, and analyze their job's components. Credibility reinforcement can be achieved by using these five components and their respective strategies. Ensuring that employees believe their institution to be a credible one is a vital concern when renewing the healthcare organization. If employees feel they are part of an organization that cannot "take care of business," they will not contribute fully to its most important mission, providing the best healthcare possible to the customer/patient.

Leadership Roles for the Renewal Process

The essential leadership roles that the healthcare manager must fulfill during the renewal process are shown in Figure 6.2. These duties should be familiar to anyone acquainted with popular, established leadership and

Figure 6.2   Leadership Roles for the Renewal Process

Facilitator	*Enlightener*
Communicator	Visionary
Advocate	Mentor
Focal point	Counselor
Investigator	Developer
Voice of reason and validation	Role model
Sounding board	Presenter
Encourager	*Activator*
Listener	Planner
Perceiver	Arbitrator
Energizer	Orchestrator
Rewarder	"Closer"
Legislator	Monitor
Coach	Innovator

management roles, but any healthcare leader undertaking a renewal effort should reflect on this figure during the process. Though familiar, however, some of the roles contained in the matrix merit specific discussion.

The healthcare manager must be both a *listener* and a *perceiver* throughout the renewal process. The difference between the two is that a listener understands *what* a staff member is saying, while a perceiver understands *why* the staff member is saying it. The leader must be able to do both. Understanding the motive behind communication is a leadership responsibility, as has been discussed, especially during the renewal process when fear is pervasive.

The leader must be an *encourager* throughout the change process and fulfill every variation of this role from empowerer to rewarder. The leader must stridently encourage creativity and initiative at every opportunity. He or she must also be forthright and resolute when confronting, managing, or removing "nonplayers." This is related, of course, to the role of leader as a coach, an analogy to an athletic coach who must motivate forty different players in forty different ways. Similarly, leaders must likewise know their players and how to inspire and motivate them.

Finally, during the renewal process, the leader must be an *advocate* of three related commodities: First, he or she must always advocate the need for positivity; second, leaders must advocate the needs of their staff to obtain the necessary resources needed for success; and third, the leader must resolutely advocate the needs of the customer/patient.

RENEWAL STRATEGIES

The renewal process is the most overlooked phase of the entire transformation effort. While many healthcare organizations put a high premium on rightsizing—along with the reconstruction effort—the renewal process is possibly the most critical stage of reorganization. When renewing, the institution actually reinvests its resources and rededicates itself to the customer/patient. In this chapter, we will discuss several essential renewal strategies that are vital not only to the success of the renewal process, but of the entire reorganization.

Ideally, the renewal process increases organizational affiliation and unity, regenerates pride in the organization, heightens recognition efforts, elevates work satisfaction, and reestablishes trust between managers and employees. By using the strategies that will be presented throughout this chapter, the renewed healthcare organization can achieve all of these goals.

Building Affiliation and Unity

Healthcare employees must feel as though their organization is, indeed, "playing to win." Most employees are motivated by a sense that their institution is doing all it can to meet the needs of the customer/patient. Providing excellent healthcare is of great importance to the average healthcare employee.

In the renewed institution, employees may be fearful that the organization cannot provide this exemplary care. Therefore, the institution must make every effort possible to create a sense of strong affiliation and unity throughout the staff. The best way to do this is for the organization to stress five objectives:

1. restate the basic mission, values, and objectives of the organization;
2. pragmatically describe how it will provide healthcare on a daily basis;
3. reinvest in community relations;
4. make concerted efforts to highlight the successes and "wins" of the renewed organization; and
5. create a renewed allegiance between the organization and each staff member.

In this section, we will discuss eight essential strategies to achieve these five objectives.

1. **Credo.** The credo statement is a review of the institution's basic beliefs. Beyond the basic mission statement, the credo should list the renewed organization's objectives, review its core values, and restate its commitment to the customer/patient. As demonstrated in Figure 7.1, the credo is a basic set of statements that reflects the organization's beliefs—not only from a traditional perspective but also with a focus toward the future.

The credo should be written using input from employees, community members, and management. In the author's experience, the most well-received credo statements have been those that reflect sentiments commonly held by both managers and employees. While focus groups can offer valid input, more valuable suggestions can usually be elicited from staff by management. Simply by asking staff members "What is more important to you in your daily responsibilities?", a manager should be able to collect five to ten answers; from this, the organization can collect the employees' common beliefs, and the foundation of the credo statement can be established.

Emblazened with the organization's logo—and printed on parchment-style paper in the institution's colors—the credo should be framed and posted at all employee entry points, patient service areas, and other

Figure 7.1 Sample Credo

As Members of the Coastal Healthcare Network, We Believe:
➡ Our Reputation is Based on Trust and Pride.
➡ Our Commitment to Our Community is Our Guiding Inspiration.
➡ Nobody Succeeds in Our Organization Unless We *All* Succeed.
➡ Quality Is More Than a Cliché, It Is How We Do Our Job Every Day.
➡ Caring and Compassion Are Our Hallmarks.

areas where it can be readily observed. Doing this is a direct sign to patients and employees alike that the organization is serious in its commitment and that the credo is more than just words—it is a way of doing business on a daily basis.

2. **Book of values/Staff handbook.** The credo should be supplemented by an organizational handbook or a book that lists the organization's essential values. In addition to reflecting the organization's core values, the handbook should list performance criteria, which in turn, can be used when selecting new employees, deciding which employees will receive promotions and transfers, and when evaluating organizational performance (Lombardi 1988, 1993).

The book of values not only supplements the credo, but attests to how the organization will serve the customer/patient. Put simply, it is a set of guidelines for *how* the institution pursues its mission of taking care of the customer/patient. As with the credo statement, the handbook should be professionally printed, replete with the organization's logo and color scheme.

In the author's experience, the most effective organizational handbooks have featured photographs of actual staff members conducting their daily work. Pictures of individuals working on the cafeteria training line are just as essential to the organizational handbook as photos of individuals working in the emergency room—it reinforces the institution's belief that the work of the cafeteria employee is just as necessary as that of emergency room nurse. Themes such as allegiance, compassion, dignity, respect, and quality should also be incorporated in the organizational handbook. Each page should have a value, clearly defined, and supplemented by at least five supporting criteria, as depicted in Figure 7.2.

Figure 7.2 Sample Page of Values Criteria

Adaptability
Shows a proven ability to perform well under changing conditions, high stress, and adverse physical conditions; can relate to varied personalities and absorb new methods with excellent practical results.
→ Is willing to expand on original duties, wants to contribute and learn as much as possible to enhance performance.
→ Has previous successful adaptations to significant change, i.e., new manager, new product, new approaches, etc.
→ Shows consistent past performance under adversity and/or major negative change.
→ Demonstrates the ability to work with a wide spectrum of people.
→ Maintains a high level of achievement under high stress/pressure.

The handbook should be presented to each staff member, as well as to each new employee. Many organizations have used the handbook effectively when conducting their new-staff orientation program. The presentation of the institution's values, and a comprehensive review of *how* it operates individually and collectively, is vital not only to a renewed organization but to *any* healthcare facility operating under the pressures of constant change.

3. **Community education.** The renewed healthcare institution should not only use the credo and handbook internally, but as the foundation of a community education process, as well. Because many customer/patients truly believe that they are not only stakeholders but investors in their local healthcare institution, their fear and apprehension following rightsizing and reconstruction can match that of the institution's employees. Thus, every effort should be made to educate the community member about the renewed organization. Publishing and distributing the credo and handbook to the community is an effective first step in enlightening the customer/patients and reassuring them that their healthcare needs will be met fully and effectively.

Community education is not solely the responsibility of the public relations office or the CEO. In a real sense, staff members become ambassadors to the community and should be charged with the responsibility of educating their friends, neighbors, and family members about the renewed organization's daily workings. Whenever possible, staff members should educate the community, including prepared presentations at the Rotary Club, for example, as well as impromptu, informal conversations at barbecues, picnics, and church events.

Certainly, formal events such as open houses can help educate the community; in fact, an open house is almost a mandatory event, if for no other reason than to demonstrate to customer/patients that the organization has not changed so much that their basic healthcare needs will not be met. Health fairs can also educate the community as well as offer screening and testing procedures. Similarly, the institution should also support "career day" events at local schools, not only to spark an interest in health careers among students but also to provide general awareness about the renewed organization.

4. **House rules.** As we have discussed, rightsizing and reconstruction should provide more comprehensive healthcare services to the customer/patient; to this end, the renewed organization should publish a set of "house rules," which become the responsibility of every employee. These rules could include, but are not limited to, the following:

1. When someone asks for directions to a particular part of the facility, do not tell them where to go, take them there.
2. Never say, "I don't know." Immediately find someone who will answer the question.
3. Never say, "It's not my job." Find the individual whose job it is.
4. Treat the fortieth person you deal with today as well as you treated the first person you treated today.
5. Focus on each patient as a source of motivation and inspiration.
6. Make certain that your work area is always clean, professional, and safe.
7. Extend every small decency necessary and needed at any time.
8. Treat your colleagues as well as you treat the patient.
9. Remember always that you are our organization, and your conduct is a living personification of our organization.
10. Demonstrate compassion, sensitivity, and perceptiveness in everything you do when you are on the campus.

These rules are not only a set of standards for conduct but supplement the credo and organizational handbook of values. Because most health-care professionals practice these standards anyway, they act as positive reinforcement to the majority of staff members.

5. **New "labels."** Some renewed healthcare organizations give themselves, as well as some internal divisions, a new title. This is a good idea, provided that the new "labels" do not create confusion, or worse, spread fear throughout the community. For example, if the customer/patient does not recognize the new label, or it makes the customer/patient think that the organization has been "bought out," the label can clearly do more harm than good.

A new label can help the renewed organization reestablish its identity with additional strength. For example, if a renewed hospital calls itself a "Medical Center," the community gets the impression that the organization has actually gotten "bigger and stronger," and can provide more services. Likewise, if a hospital has acquired an outpatient clinic, or has merged with a home for the aging, the hospital can change its name from "Community Hospital" to "Community Health System," again reinforcing the impression that it has become "bigger and stronger."

If a new label is adopted, the organization's logo and colors should remain the same. This helps to maintain at least one point of consistency in the perception of the customer/patient. Conversely, if an organization does not change its name, the renewal process might present an excellent opportunity to change the logo to a more progressive scheme or incorporate new signage and other visual features that might demonstrate the renewal in a positive light.

6. **CEO report.** The CEO report can be a strong motivating force in increasing organizational affiliation, and it should be published at the three critical junctures of the reorganization process. First is during the rightsizing effort, when it can explain what rightsizing will entail, as well as the rationale and need for it. The second juncture is during the reconstruction effort, when the new organizational structure is introduced; the CEO can use the report to highlight the new model's benefits.

The third logical point for a CEO report is during organizational renewal; at that point, the CEO report should contain these six features:

1. an express appreciation to all staff members for their participation and support of the rightsizing and restructuring effort;
2. a basic review of the organization, complete with positive points, such as financial progress, or other indicators that demonstrate that the organization is indeed "on the right track" in the reorganization process;
3. the introduction of the credo, organizational handbook, and new label—if any—to increase support for them;
4. a review of the institution's current status, to include positive indicators of performance;
5. a brief assessment of the organization's immediate future, given its new structure, to help staff comprehend and support the changes; and
6. a long-range perspective from the CEO on the organization's growth and progress, perhaps supported by a timeline depiction (Lombardi 1996).

The CEO report should be delivered to each employee and augmented whenever possible by the comments of each supervisor and manager. Moreover, the CEO report should be distributed appropriately to community members and presented in conjunction with CEO briefings, town hall meetings, community action nights, and other gatherings in which this essential six-part message can be conveyed.

7. **Celebrate all "wins."** Every supervisor and manager in the renewed organization must celebrate "wins." Because of their desire to be perfectionists, healthcare managers and supervisors have a proclivity for focusing on what is wrong, not what is right. This can be devastating in the renewal process, when fear and apprehension are prevalent in the workplace. Therefore, the manager and supervisor should look for opportunities to highlight and celebrate wins; this demonstrates the work team's ability to provide better healthcare services under the aegis of the renewed institutional structure.

Celebrating the wins can take on several shapes. For example, by comparing last year's results with this year's—given, of course, that this year's results are positive—a clear analysis can be provided that shows the benefit of the renewed organization. Comparing organizational success with the failings of a competing organization, which has not reconstructed, is another way to celebrate success. The use of a timeline, as we have discussed throughout this book, can also chart organizational progress and increase team allegiance.

Moreover, citing an individual's strong work contribution by the manager can go a long way toward "celebrating the wins." This again is the healthcare leader's responsibility. Further, publicly citing praise from customer/patients describing the specific action of an employee that resulted in better healthcare is also a "win" that merits celebration. Perhaps most substantially, the healthcare leader who asks employees, "What have we been doing *right* recently?" is setting the framework for the discussion of a win that is clearly recognized, valid in the eyes of all employees, and reflects the renewed organization's success.

8. **"Garment gimmicks."** Using t-shirts, windbreakers, and other garments bearing an institution's logo, its new motto, and other features can seem trivial at first. Recently, however, "brand name" garments have become not only fashionable but a major fad throughout American society. Certain sportswear manufacturers sell more garments with their logo than those they manufacture with the logo of professional sports teams.

With this in mind, using garments that have the renewed organization's logo and other features can be a powerful marketing tool as well as a component of the affiliation process. Many institutions have used clothing, hats, golf towels, and other garments not only to demonstrate their new logo and name to the community but to increase employee awareness of the labels. The garments can be given out meritoriously, such as an award for employee-of-the-month or other recognition strategies, or simply distributed to all staff members. Using these garments should not be discounted, as they have tremendous impact on staff members, as well as their friends and neighbors throughout the community.

These eight affiliation strategies can help create a sense of allegiance among all staff members and, used in concert, can set the pace and raise new expectations for all staff members as the renewed organization moves toward a progressive future.

Regenerating Pride

The success of the renewed organization rests on its ability to create a sense of renewed pride among employees. This pride must be founded on the institution's traditional strengths and bolstered by its new abilities. In this section, we will describe eight practical strategies to foster pride in the renewed organization.

1. **Board summit.** In order to engage all levels of leadership in renewal effort, a board summit should be conducted as a forum to discuss the new institution's direction and strategies with the board of directors. The word "summit" should be used instead of "retreat," as the organization is moving forward and upward, not "retreating" from its competitive environment. The board summit should be a special event, specifically scheduled to discuss the renewed organization's intents.

At the summit, a set of strategic initiatives should be discussed. The CEO should take primary responsibility to express the institution's specific goals and to suggest ways in which the board can best support the renewed organization. While the input of all board members is valued throughout the renewal process, the specific actions taken by board members to support the new organization are even more essential. This would include their efforts in community outreach, increasing community awareness of the renewed organization, and committing whatever resources possible—financial or otherwise—toward the renewal process.

At the summit, all board members should understand three critical facts. First, the organization intends to concentrate on the future, not the past. Board members should recommit themselves to the future of the organization and not use the past as an inappropriate basis for understanding or formulating future strategy. Second, all board members should understand that "nobody will win unless we all win," and therefore their participation is needed as first-guessers, active players, and proponents of the new system—not as retroactive, regressive, second-guessers. Finally, all board members should understand that the renewal process is permanent, and that change will be a constant factor as the organization moves forward. With these facts as standards, all board members should then be encouraged to participate in the renewed organization.

The summit's purpose is not only to increase organizational pride but also to enlist the board's support in future action. The renewal process is a prime opportunity to reconstruct boards, add new board members, or perhaps remove board members who are resistant to change.

2. **Volunteer activation.** Volunteers are an essential component of any healthcare organization. They bring skills to the renewed organization, as well as their continuing commitment to its objective and mission. Unfortunately, given an institution's reconstruction and transformation, volunteers are sometimes "lost in the shuffle." As a result, their pride in the organization can wane, and their participation in the organizational scheme can diminish.

Volunteer activation takes two forms. First, education should be provided to all volunteer groups throughout the reorganization—particularly during the renewal process. A clear picture should be presented about the future objectives of the organization and the mission of the renewed organization. Additionally, the particular role of each volunteer—and from a general perspective, the role of the entire volunteer corps—should be defined clearly to eliminate any apprehension and fear.

Second, each volunteer's abilities should be scrutinized and fully examined in the interests of fully optimizing his or her potential contribution. For example, if a volunteer has particular marketing skills, these skills can be used to create a new logo, signage, and any other marketing aspects of affiliation. If other volunteers are retired teachers, for instance, they can be consulted when creating a day care center. In short, the renewal process offers a natural opportunity not only to reinvest volunteer pride in the organization but to reassess specific volunteer skills.

3. **"Fan mail" posting.** Investing fifty dollars to erect a bulletin board on which to post "fan mail" might be the most intelligent expenditure a CEO can make during the renewal process. On this bulletin board, letters from patients, family members, and other healthcare organizational stakeholders can be posted for review by all staff. The bulletin board should be placed in a prominent location, such as the employee cafeteria. Whenever the CEO receives a letter lauding organizational or individual action—particularly action that occurred because of the reorganization process—the correspondence should be posted immediately on the bulletin board.

Likewise, any fan mail received by individual department leaders or unit supervisors should be posted as well. This correspondence is equally important, and relevant in the eyes of all staff members. Furthermore, any newspaper articles or positive local press coverage should also be posted.

The fan mail bulletin board is a simple idea, and is extremely effective if well managed. Correspondence should be placed on the bulletin board in a timely manner. When new material is added, all old correspondence should be removed. If an article or letter stays too long, "nonplayers" may think—and say—that the organization has done nothing of consequence lately. On the other hand, certain correspondence that is timeless should be placed on the bulletin board, perhaps under a "Hallmarks of Our Success" section. The fan mail bulletin board can not only increase pride, but also affiliation and respect for the healthcare organization among staff.

4. **"The big event."** The renewed organization can use a "big event" to launch renewal strategies, such as a new employee credo, organizational handbook, and logo. The event can be a holiday party, employee picnic, or perhaps a founder's day celebration.

The big event should be used as an educational opportunity to increase awareness of the renewed organization. Accordingly, a presentation, in the form of a short speech, is mandatory on the part of the organization's CEO. Additionally, distributing "garment gimmicks" is also important. Naturally, food should become part of the process as well! An employee picnic, holiday party, or other organizational event where there is food provides a relaxed setting for discussion about the organization, as well as the opportunity for all staff to renew acquaintances with colleagues and community members.

For the renewed organization, the use of a new benchmark might be appropriate for the "big event." For example, Founder's Day is usually celebrated by major corporations but not by healthcare facilities. By researching when a community hospital was founded, for example, and by celebrating that "anniversary day" in concert with the launch of the renewed organization, a new benchmark can be established that can be used in subsequent years as a new "special day" that all staff members and stakeholders can anticipate.

5. **Organizational surveys.** Using organizational surveys is essential to any healthcare organization, regardless of the particular business circumstances (Lombardi 1993). In a renewed organization, however, survey results can become a specific source of pride. An organizational survey, for example, that evaluates organizational effectiveness, departmental efficiency, leadership strength, job scope, and other critical issues is a useful tool—particularly when used as a comparison between the old organization and the new one.

With this in mind, it might be useful for the renewed organization to conduct a survey immediately after launching the renewed healthcare organization. Then, six months later, a comparison survey should be taken. Regardless of the specific outcomes, surveys of this type can become a clear, direct indicator to organizational leadership on the relative efficiency of the reorganization process.

The change readiness index and other similar surveys should also be used. In organizations where leadership is fearful that the survey results might actually worsen after the renewal—a natural occurrence, even under the best of circumstances, given fear and apprehension—another, more specific type of survey might be used. This could be a simple open-ended questionnaire with the following questions:

1. What can we be doing in the next six months to get better?
2. The three biggest things I have learned during the past six months are: _____ ;
3. In order to be successful, we must all understand: _____ ; and

4. In order to make our organization successful, my colleagues and I must always: _____ .

Using these basic open-ended questions can generate positive data that can be utilized pragmatically by staff members, and will reflect a well-spring of pride in the organization.

6. **Quarterly reviews.** Every three months, each department should chart significant quantitative results, which can be posted using numbers that reflect significant gains. They can also reflect percentages—both positive and negative—that affect organizational performance. Additionally, time efficiency and cost effectiveness should also be charted each quarter.

These quarterly reviews should be done in concert between the manager and his or her respective work team. Quarterly reviews can be a tremendous tool in assessing departmental progress, and they can be further used as rallying points for renewed commitment to departmental achievements. If used artfully throughout the organization, the results of all the quarterly reviews can be combined into a comprehensive institutional review, which can be included in the annual report. When published, the report can generate organizational pride and redefine staff commitment.

7. **Timelines.** As discussed extensively, timelines should be used by all managers throughout the reorganization process—especially during the renewal process. The timeline for the renewal process can commence on the date the "big event" takes place and continue to the end of the calendar year, conclusion of the fiscal year, or the first anniversary of the "big event" (e.g., the next Founder's Day). Timelines are an illustrative tool, easily composed, and extremely open-ended and receptive to employee input. Timelines should be easily recognizable by the employee, and highly motivating. Timeline construction can either be intricate—listing specific details of a certain project—or more general in scope (Lombardi 1996).

8. **Annual report.** The annual report, which differs from the CEO report in that it focuses on the entire organization, is mandatory during the renewal process. As the name suggests, the annual report is a report developed by the CEO that reviews organizational performance in its initial year and then in every subsequent year. If all managers have endeavored to create quarterly reviews—and have composed timelines on their work team's progress—the data collected makes an overall annual report a natural and efficient process.

The annual report should contain a letter from the CEO to all staff members and stakeholders that should briefly review organizational progress from a financial, operational, and personnel standpoint. The report should then list specific timelines indicating past progress and future plans. This report should then be distributed to all staff to promote a sense of pride in current and previous accomplishments.

Regenerating pride is crucial to a renewed organization. Pride is a major motivating factor, and critical to the performance of every healthcare professional. Using these simple strategies can provide the direction for future action and a review of previous accomplishments, which not only generates pride but ensures exemplary performance.

Recognizing Performance

Recognition is perhaps the most time-honored motivational strategy. Honoring achievement, accomplishment, and contribution is always important, but even more essential in the renewed healthcare organization. As a certain amount of uncertainty enters the workplace regarding duties and responsibilities, the need for recognition becomes particularly strong.

In this section, we will review recognition strategies that are not only essential to the immediate renewal process but also to overall organizational efficiency. Each strategy is clear-cut, user-friendly, and ready to implement in any institution.

1. **"Team of the month."** Many healthcare organizations have traditionally recognized an employee of the month, who is usually honored with a photograph in the hospital's lobby and in the employee newsletter. In a renewed organization, however, where teamwork and allegiance are essential ingredients of success, the employee-of-the-month notion can be strengthened with the addition of a team of the month.

The team of the month would be a work team that has made a particular noteworthy contribution to the organization. In a renewed institution, this can be a terrific asset for generating not only recognition but pride, affiliation, and other essential elements of success. In a product-line organization, for example, a team of the month could be a component of a product line that did not exist in the previous organization. They should be celebrated, like the employee of the month, with a photograph in a prominent location in the facility as well as a mention in the employee newsletter. Moreover, the team can be featured in an annual report, quarterly review, and other communication devices throughout the organization.

The team of the month should be selected based on these criteria:

1. contribution to the organization;
2. service to the customer/patient;

3. adherence to the new "house rules" of the organization, handbook of values, and other new criteria;
4. teamwork, allegiance, and peer support throughout the team; and
5. the use of existing resources to accomplish the mission of the team.

The selection of the team of the month sends a clear message to all staff that performance is not only valued and recognized, but celebrated as part of the new organization.

2. **"Thank you times three."** The most underused words in the current American healthcare management lexicon are "thank you." A score of organizational surveys, employee input meetings, and other communication exercises conducted by the author suggest that this simple recognition strategy is woefully neglected by most healthcare managers and supervisors. Accordingly, the renewed organization should stress a rededication to these two simple words.

There are three aspects a manager must consider when saying "thank you." First, the manager should acknowledge the individual's action that benefited the customer/patient. The supervisor should also express appreciation on the part of the institution, as the individual's action helped the organization "look good." Finally, the manager should express appreciation on behalf of the work team, which profited by the individual's exemplary action.

Individuals who are thanked in this manner will perceive themselves more appreciated, esteemed, and recognized in the eyes of their managers. Further, the individuals will also recognize that their actions are also regarded favorably by the organization, the customer/patient, and the individual team. For the overwhelming majority of healthcare employees, "thank you times three" will not only be a positive motivator but the most positive manifestation of the renewed organization as it affects their professional lives.

3. **Newsletters.** Most healthcare facilities have a newsletter that is circulated regularly. Using this newsletter to spread positive information will help any healthcare organization. Many institutions have done this to present information about recent promotions, attainment of professional certifications and licenses, and other notable achievements of staff members and managers.

Additionally, newsletters can be used to publicize organizational accomplishments. For example, percentages and significant numbers that indicate increases in positive performances can be presented. For example, a newsletter can highlight an institution's increase in outpatient admissions, patient satisfaction, and the quality of emergency room service, along with quantitative documentation.

Newsletters can also highlight community-based events such as health fairs, as well as the introduction of new medical services to benefit the customer/patient. To be fully effective, the newsletter should be circulated not only through the healthcare organization but also throughout the surrounding community. Many progressive healthcare organizations have circulated their newsletter at places of worship, community centers, schools, and other such locations.

Because newsletters are widely read in the healthcare organization, they are essential components of any institutional recognition strategy. By using them as such, as well as a source of information, the facility can openly celebrate its individual and collective "wins."

4. **Video production.** Virtually every American healthcare professional has access to a VCR unit. Both at home and at work, the video has joined television as the "sixth sense of America." Accordingly, every renewed healthcare organization with a good story to tell should use its video capacity to the maximum. Most healthcare organizations have a capacity to produce videotapes in-house, and these tapes can educate and train staff on medical procedures and other technically based information.

The renewed institution can produce and distribute a videotape based on its recent successes. In essence, the videotape would become a video version of the organization's annual report, replete with information about improved services and individual success stories.

For instance, if an organization has moved primarily to a decentralized model, in which clinics and outpatient services are now the main focus, a video can be produced that describes the various clinics and outpatient services. This narrative can also review the recent history of the outpatient clinic, follow a patient's progress, and perhaps document the staff's experiences. In another example, an organization with a new outpatient clinic can produce a video that documents its evolution, as well as feature personal stories and a positive presentation of the new facility's capabilities.

Organizational videos can be extremely adaptable assets to the renewed organization. They can be freely shared by organizational members, customer/patients, and other stakeholders and can contribute to the institution's overall organizational communication strategy. Moreover, video presents a relatively cost-efficient, time-effective method for delivering an important, positive message to all organizational stakeholders.

5. **Flexible benefits.** In a renewed organization, introducing a flexible benefits plan can clearly recognize the efforts of an institution's "steady"

and "superstar" employees. This program allows employees to select the type of supplemental benefits they need.

Among many healthcare professionals, benefits have become more important than monetary compensation. Recognizing the reality that most healthcare organizations are currently undergoing a period of financial distress, typical American healthcare workers recognize that their salary will not rise appreciably in the coming years. They are, however, aware of their benefits, and they rely on the organization to provide them, which are essential to their quality of life. Accordingly, the healthcare organization can recognize good employees through a flexible benefits package in which benefits are incrementally increased based on good performance. For example, if an employee performs well on an annual performance evaluation, he or she can request an increase in medical benefits, a decrease in the deductible on their dental benefits, or perhaps extra consideration for day care or other such benefits. If the organization cannot afford benefits, which are increasingly expensive, additional time off and an increase in vacation days can become a viable option.

Flexible benefits recognize good employees in two ways: First, the institution clearly expresses to the employee that it appreciates his or her service and thus wants to provide additional benefits to enhance the employee's quality of life. Second, by its very nature, flexible benefits connote clearly to the employee that the organization trusts him or her fully and renders its trust by providing a favorable benefits package.

6. **Change management education.** Every American healthcare organization will undergo intense change in the next few years because of rapidly developing technology, increasing public scrutiny, and the volatile state of healthcare delivery. It is incumbent upon the organization to recognize that change is a fact of life and provide its employees with the education necessary to cope with it. In addition to being a recognition strategy, change management education is also an essential component of staff development.

Change management education should be presented not only to managers and medical staff but to every staff member. Because change affects a housekeeper, maintenance worker, and security guard as dramatically as a heart surgeon, the opportunity to learn how to manage change must be given to everyone. The basic components of change management education should center on five essential areas:

1. why healthcare is changing rapidly;
2. what the customer/patient expects during times of change;
3. the defining values and elements of a healthcare organization during change;

4. how to cope with the change process individually; and

5. how to make change a positive experience for the entire organization through interdependence, proaction, and organizational unity.

By addressing these concerns, in a three-hour seminar for all employees, the healthcare organization can not only provide insightful education but also recognize the contributions of individuals throughout the change process.

7. **Compensation programs.** Immediately following an organization's restructuring effort, it must redefine its compensation system. Recent financial constraints have limited many institutions' ability to offer more than standard cost-of-living adjustments. In a renewed organization, however, opportunities exist to alter the compensation strategy in a way that recognizes the contributing members and provides an incentive for exemplary service.

Naturally, many compensation systems are premised on performance. The renewed organization should therefore adopt a criterion-based performance evaluation system, in which individuals are assessed relative to job component achievement, work quality standards, attitude, interpersonal skills, and team orientation. Individuals should be appraised relative to their performance that is clearly "above and beyond" the call of duty, and the evaluation must also incorporate new programs and services that the employee introduced or implemented either individually or with a work team (Lombardi 1988, 1992).

Once this criterion-based performance evaluation system has been installed, the organization can turn its attention to a merit-based incentive compensation program. Based on the outcomes of the individual performance evaluations, the staff member can be rewarded by any one of these:

1. an increase in base pay;

2. an increase in "step" increases, relative to the normal pay range;

3. a reward of additional vacation days;

4. a reward of an organizationally based bonus, such as a gainsharing or a merit bonus; or

5. a reward of an individual bonus, based on a percentage of the employee's individual compensation level.

Merit-based compensation systems are essential for long-term organizational success, as good employees must be rewarded and negative employees must be redressed and ultimately removed. Regardless of the type of organizational merit-based incentive compensation system used, negative employees, who clearly have performed at a "below expectations" level on their performance evaluations, must be put on immediate probation for three months to resolve their performance problems or be terminated immediately. A solid criterion-based performance evaluation system gives the institution the ability not only to reward and recognize the good employees, but also to remove the employees who are not interested in the organization's progress and prosperity.

8. **Comparison/contrast.** This strategy basically asks the question, "What would happen if we did not change?" That is, the comparison/contrast method compares the organization's present strategy to its previous one, and contrasts its current success to the hypothetical situation of never having undertaken any change at all. Using this method gives a renewed healthcare organization a subtle but effective method of recognition: By focusing on the institution's current success—while acknowledging a few problems and pressing needs—leadership can provide all stakeholders with an honest assessment of the facility's current status. This status, however, becomes more positive and hopeful when contrasted against what could have happened had the institution not changed. Employees can see that their efforts have prevented the facility from failing or stagnating.

Comparison/contrast can be used at every level of the organization, but it must begin at the executive suite. The healthcare leader who uses timelines and other communication techniques to demonstrate the difference between the previous organization and the renewed one—or the current organization as opposed to one that did not change—sets an example for every leader throughout the chain of command. Department heads and supervisors can use comparison/contrast to analyze specific elements within their divisions. With the ever-accelerating pace of healthcare, a period of one year can represent a dramatic comparison/contrast in these discussions.

The results of a comparison/contrast exercise should be spread by every communication venue discussed in this chapter. If the institution recognizes first that it is better off than it was previously and, moreover, demonstrates its recognition and appreciation to employees in making that successful transition possible, future success becomes the product of a natural wellspring of trust and pride from the current organization.

Increasing Work Satisfaction

Satisfaction is a primary motivator of a healthcare professional. The ability to practice one's craft and apply all of one's powers—mental, physical, and spiritual—to help fellow human beings in pain and need is the essence of satisfaction as it relates to any healthcare professional.

In this section, we will describe nine strategies a healthcare organization can use to impart a greater sense of satisfaction to each staff member.

1. **Job component review.** In the renewed organization, every employee will have new responsibilities, accountabilities, and job tasks. The organization must immediately recognize this and provide the opportunity for each staff member to review his or her individual job role.

The use of a job component review, as specified in earlier chapters of this book, must be implemented from a positive viewpoint. As discussed earlier, employees should list all of their essential job components and assign an approximate time value, weighted value, and overall performance value to each one. This can be done together with the manager or supervisor, or independently by the employee pending subsequent review, ratification, and approval by the immediate supervisor or manager. Employees should use their previous job description as a foundation for the review, but the previous description should act as no more than a cursory guide to the process. Instead, employees should consider a "typical day" given their job roles in the renewed organization and construct the review accordingly.

Reviewing job components can help establish a performance review system that is criterion-based and job specific, as described in the previous section. Furthermore, the employee and manager alike can use the job component review as a guide for action in the renewed organization and as a building block for heightening performance effectiveness.

2. **"Back to the basics" program.** A "back to the basics" program can help assuage employee fear—which is always present during change—and refocus the employee on the critical, essential elements of healthcare delivery. The best way to implement a "back to the basics" program is to use a "patient-focus" set of practices, which must be simple and clear to offset the complexity within the healthcare business arena.

There are three such "patient-focused" practices:

1. Focus on one patient a day, whom you observe as you arrive at work, and dedicate all of your efforts toward helping that person to get better.
2. Recognize that patient care is everyone's job and that all of your daily efforts are directed toward helping the patient.
3. Any time is a good time to provide a suggestion to help the patient receive quality care efficiently and effectively.

These three practices must be articulated and demonstrated throughout the facility. In many organizations, these three rules have been attached to the back of employee ID badges or printed on posters placed in employee lunch areas. Because most employees find a sense of satisfaction in helping a patient, this focus on patients can not only allay fears but further that sense of satisfaction.

3. **Educational needs analysis.** Most healthcare professionals value education as a key component of their worklife. In many instances, unfortunately, the education and training budget is the first casualty of a restructured organization, which is unfortunate: In times of change, apprehension, and fear, education *must* be provided to enlighten individuals about change and how it will affect them.

In addition to the change management educational sessions discussed earlier, the healthcare facility must ensure that employee educational needs will not be sacrificed during restructuring and renewal. In fact, the renewal process is a perfect opportunity for the organization to recommit itself to employee education and development. The best way to demonstrate this new commitment is by conducting a training and educational needs analysis.

This analysis uses a simple questionnaire to determine the current educational needs and developmental opportunities that exist for each individual employee. Furthermore, the needs analysis can also collect information on who can provide employee training by having a second part of the questionnaire where individuals are asked to identify areas of specific expertise and subject areas in which they feel qualified and comfortable to act as instructors. The results of both parts of this needs analysis—the education required and the education that can be provided by current staff—should then be collected to form the basis for a cohesive training and development plan.

4. **Personnel development plans.** After completing job component reviews, constructing personnel development plans is essential to maintaining a sense of satisfaction throughout the organization. These plans basically highlight each staff member's technical strengths, development needs, promotability, and long-term potential member. Personnel development plans can be schematic in nature (Lombardi 1992) or be a simple supplement on an organizational chart indicating individual promotability and long-term potential in that institution.

In addition to promotional opportunities, a basic developmental strategy should be formulated by the manager—with the assistance of a competent human resources or educational professional—when determining the specific developmental needs of each employee. This discourse should result in a clear developmental plan for each organizational member.

Implementing a personnel development plan can not only increase staff satisfaction, but also provide inspiration and motivation in regard to future opportunities in the organization.

5. **Ambassador programs.** Each staff member is in essence an ambassador to the community. As healthcare organizations undergo a rapid amount of change, it is vital that community members do not lose trust in the institution or feel that it is either "too good" or "too bad" for them. That is, if an organization begins to specialize, consumers with more typical needs might feel that it is now "too good" to address them. On the other hand, if the institution undergoes a negative change, such as massive downsizing, consumers might feel that it is "too bad"—that is, poorly equipped—to handle their pressing healthcare concerns.

Accordingly, each staff member must act as an ambassador to the community. In formal settings, such as health fairs and lectures at local schools, employees can present information about health careers, as well as the current focus of their employing organization. In a more informal setting, individuals can "talk up" the healthcare facility, if they are prepared and educated to its current capacities and capabilities.

Moreover, staff members must understand that they are ambassadors to the community in their everyday actions. This can be stressed through various training sessions, by implementing the programs suggested throughout this chapter and by using employee-generated data when forming strategic plans and other "patient-focus" initiatives.

6. **"Fact sheets."** "Fact sheets" are communication instruments that briefly highlight the institution's accomplishments, its capacity for providing healthcare, and its features. Fact sheets can present information about specialized services as well as more traditional healthcare services, such as maternity and emergency room services.

As the name implies, fact sheets are simple, one-page descriptions of the organization that reaffirm its continuing community commitment as well as its new capacities. As illustrated in Figure 7.3, fact sheets are easy to construct and can be a useful tool in the ambassador program.

Fact sheets should be written with employee input and feedback. Furthermore, they can provide an optimum sense of employee satis-

Figure 7.3   Fact Sheet for a VA Hospital

Fact: Seventy-one percent of VA facilities are affiliated with medical teaching organizations. Only 17 percent of civilian facilities have such arrangements.

Fact: Ninety-two percent of the physicians practicing in the United States trained at a VA facility at some point in their education, although the VA only employs 2 percent of the nation's physicians.

Fact: Telepathology, open-air MRIs, and other innovations were first used in VA facilities.

VA Healthcare: Better Than Most, and Better Than You Think

faction if they are constructed at each department level—that is, each specific department develops a "fact sheet" detailing its specific services and capabilities. These fact sheets can be distributed to all incoming patients over a six-month period following a reconstruction to allay the fears of organizational stakeholders and clearly demonstrate the benefit of reconstruction and renewal.

7. **Redefinition strategies.** Redefining a position based on new job components can be a useful tool in organizational renewal. Likewise, redefining a department can lead to a greater sense of satisfaction not only for departmental members, but potentially for the entire institution. For example, if a laboratory component and a radiology capacity are combined in an organizational restructure, the department of diagnostic services might not only want to streamline job positions but also redefine each position with new titles and perhaps a new rank structure. Supplemented by an accurate fact sheet, redefinition can help increase satisfaction in several ways.

First, many healthcare professionals think they do not receive enough credit for what they do. Accordingly, if a job component review is conducted, and a position is redefined, the staff member will immediately see the benefit of organizational renewal. In another sense, if the entire department feels it is not given enough credit for its effort, a similar redefinition—perhaps with a new title—can again demonstrate an immediate positive impact of renewal.

It is essential to note that redefinition is not the same as renaming— that is, imposing a new title arbitrarily. Redefinition must be augmented with an actual review of new position components and a redefining of the entire scope of the services provided.

8. **General employee education.** Employee education that is general in nature and does not specifically deal with technical issues can also be a contributor to organizational and individual satisfaction after the restructuring process. As we have discussed, specific technical training, as well as education on the change process, are essential topics for employee education.

However, from a more general perspective, employee education should be broadened to provide staff with the expertise needed for dealing in a competitive healthcare business arena. These topics can be easily incorporated into employee educational sessions:

- customer service strategies;
- negotiation skills;
- conflict resolution;
- interpersonal support systems;

- communication skills; and
- professional etiquette.

9. **Management education.** Similarly, management education also contributes to satisfaction and does not have to be confined to change management and specific technical applications. Many healthcare organizations have found that the renewal process is aided by educating managers in these topics:

- selection and hiring skills;
- performance evaluation;
- motivation;
- managing resistance to change;
- managing conflict among employees;
- managed care strategies;
- time management;
- stress management;
- increasing pride and trust among staff; and
- dealing with the "nonplayer."

As is the case with employee education, management education can be provided by a capable in-house employee or by an external expert. In either case, the education must be practical, relevant, and timely. The training sessions should ideally be short and succinct.

Renewing Trust

Following the tumultuous restructuring process, trust must be renewed between management and employees, as well as between individual managers and their staff members. In this section, we will review several techniques that the readers should implement immediately and that must become part of their everyday management approach.

1. **The Execu-gram.** A common lament of healthcare professionals during the restructuring and renewal process is "We don't receive enough communication" or "We find out about things after they happen." Obviously, communication is the most nebulous characteristic of a healthcare organization and is usually the most difficult to effect, despite management's best intentions.

In many healthcare institutions, the Execu-gram has been used successfully. Based on the Western Union Telegram Company's practice of making telegrams yellow in order to be noticed quickly in a stack of white paper, Execu-grams have been used by healthcare organizations so the senior administrator can spread information to all organizational members quickly and efficiently. The most dramatic example of this in the author's experience was the "Rainbow-gram" used by a VA facility in Hawaii.

In this instance, the facility's director used rainbow-colored paper to communicate information about:

- important new directives;
- countering rumors with facts;
- operational initiatives; and
- major changes within the organization.

By employing colored paper that will immediately capture employees' attention, and by using the Execu-gram only in cases suggested by these four criteria, communication to all members of the organization can be quick, clear, and effective.

2. **Selection system.** In a renewed organization, a structured selection system must be used when deciding all internal promotions as well as when selecting new employees. In a renewed organization that has undergone rightsizing, an open position is a valued asset. Therefore, the best candidate must be selected for the position, or trust will erode among the employee ranks.

A structured selection system looks at *what* the candidate does and *how* he or she provides healthcare daily using a set of questions. Such factors as attitudes, interpersonal skills, managerial aptitude, and team orientation must be considered (Lombardi 1988). A structured selection system must also extend to internal candidates requesting a promotion, so that the process is uniform, incorporates standards from the performance evaluation system, and again considers not only *what* the candidate does, but *how* he or she discharges professional activities on a daily basis.

3. **Communicating AMAP/ASAP.** If the healthcare leader wishes to be successful, there cannot be a void of communication. It is essential that he or she communicate as much as possible as soon as possible. There is no such thing as "overcommunication" in the modern healthcare establishment. When employees are afraid, they often lose the gist of a message or listen selectively for the information they require immediately. It is incumbent upon the healthcare leader to provide as much information as possible, even if it is sometimes redundant, as quickly as possible. Four basic rules apply here:

1. Do not assume anything regarding communication.
2. Do not worry about overcommunicating something, even if you have to repeat yourself occasionally.
3. Make certain that everyone receives the message.
4. Make sure you repeat the message at least once.

Even at the risk of being pedantic or redundant, the healthcare manager must communicate in this manner. In fact, in the interest of clarity, the healthcare leader can even apologize for appearing to be redundant and then repeat the message anyway. It is better to err on the side of overcommunication in these pressing times rather than risk undercommunication.

4. **"Nonplayer" management.** As has been mentioned, the "non-players" in the renewed organization must be addressed resolutely and forcefully. Whether through the use of a criterion-based performance evaluation, or by using the arguments discussed in the appendix, "non-players" must not be allowed to dominate the discussion in monthly meetings or to use an excessive amount of the manager's supervisory time. This initiative must be extended throughout the organization and be predominate in all work discussions.

The "nonplayers'" normal apathy and extraordinary self-focus becomes even more perilous in a renewed organization. The healthcare manager must take strides to force them to become more accountable, contrast their performance to the rest of their work group, and document their performance accordingly—in the interests of ultimately removing them from the organization. This mission must be shared throughout the chain of command, and throughout the organization, for the renewed organization to be ultimately successful. See the appendix for additional ways to manage "nonplayers."

5. **Monthly meetings.** Every manager during the renewal process, as well as the restructuring process, must hold a monthly meeting with all staff members. During this meeting, these topics should be discussed:

- the rumor of the month;
- the outstanding "steady" staff member of the month;
- the win of the month;
- the idea of the month;
- the organizational issue of the month; and
- the learning tip of the month.

If a manager does not have the time for a monthly meeting of at least fifteen minutes' duration, then he or she should not be a manager of the renewed healthcare organization. Communication is the most important factor in a renewed organization's success; consequently, monthly dialogue between the staff and manager is essential.

6. **Mistake review.** When a mistake is made, doubts about the organization's competency can quickly surface. Therefore, the leader at every level should immediately conduct a communication forum where mistakes are reviewed comprehensively and progressively.

The manager should take the lead in discussing the following four topic areas:

1. What happened?
2. Why did it happen?
3. What was learned from the mistake?
4. What will the department do next time?

After leading the discussion, the manager should review all four questions with each individual departmental member or with the group. By doing so, a strategic plan can be initiated for more adequately and competently handling a similar situation in the future, while addressing any fears and apprehension.

7. **Standards for employee input.** To build trust throughout the department—and indeed throughout the entire organization—employee input must be elicited and used appropriately at every available opportunity. However, employee input must meet five basic standards:

1. It must be *useful* given present dynamics.
2. It must be *realistic* given organizational resources.
3. It must be *appropriate* given the organization's mission and objectives.
4. It must be *needed* rather than wanted or merely desired.
5. It must be *progressive*, focusing on the future and not the past.

Many "nonplayers" complain that their input is not used. This is because it usually does not meet these five standards. By first defining these standards, and subsequently using them daily, employee input from "superstar" and "steady" employees will supersede the useless input from "nonplayers," thus building a stronger bond of trust between positive staff members and their respective managers.

8. **Communication essentials.** In all cases, managers should communicate to employees using the following five principles:

1. Here is what we need to do.
2. Here is how we are going to do it.
3. Here is when we are going to do it.
4. This is why we are going to do it.
5. Here is where we are going to start.

By using these principles, the manager can ensure that trust throughout the renewal process is bolstered by artful communication.

All of these strategies are cost effective and easy to implement, and their use can be pivotal to the success of the renewed healthcare organization.

References

Lombardi, D. N. 1988. *The Handbook of Personnel Selection and Performance Evaluation in Healthcare*. San Francisco: Jossey-Bass.

———. 1992. *Progressive Health Care Management Strategies*. Chicago: American Hospital Publishing.

———. 1993. *Handbook for the New Health Care Manager*. Chicago: American Hospital Publishing.

———. 1996. *Thriving in an Age of Change*. Chicago: Health Administration Press.

CASE STUDY: FOREST VIEW HEALTHCARE SYSTEM

The following case study is based on the author's experience in a healthcare organization that undertook the total reorganization process. In reviewing how the rightsizing, restructuring, and renewal was used in this particular case, the readers will not only gain a stronger understanding of the principles of the transition process but learn how these applications and strategies can be applied to their institutions.

The Forest View Hospital was established in 1958 to serve four suburban communities of a large midwestern city. Throughout its history, Forest View Hospital was profitable and was able to provide traditional healthcare services—such as maternity and inpatient services—to its patients/community. Partly because of this success, the institution has had only two presidents throughout its history. The first, Larry Farmer, was president from its inception until seven years ago. His successor, Lauretta Barnes, had been at the helm of the institution for seven years, but recently resigned from her position to accept a job as finance director for a nearby HMO.

The new CEO, Paul Callan, inherited an organization that although fundamentally sound lacked a clear sense of direction and stability. For example, during Barnes' tenure, the hospital suffered its first period of financial decline. For the past three years, the hospital actually lost money. Part of Callan's charter, as established by the board of directors, is to remedy this fiscal problem. This will not be an easy task, however, as the hospital has witnessed a distinct shift to outpatient services and other more "cutting-edge" healthcare services. Furthermore, it is Callan's belief that the hospital is currently somewhat overstaffed and in need of a rightsizing effort, which Barnes had avoided at all costs.

Callan has also decided that the organization has squandered over two million dollars over the past five years ostensibly to improve quality throughout the hospital: Barnes contracted a consulting firm to provide an "optimum quality program" throughout the entire organization with the intention of providing a total quality management orientation to the institution. However, the organization that provided these services, the East Delaware Consulting Corporation, charged the hospital in excess of two million dollars for its services, with little measurable gain or improvement. In reviewing quantitative indicators of quality, Callan could not find any noticeable improvement; in fact, the hospital suffered a decline in performance—especially in some sectors that were regularly reviewed by national accreditation organizations.

Another issue confronting Callan is the shift in Forest View's population. Many residents are either retirees or are approaching retirement age. These individuals, who were young parents when the hospital was founded, require different medical services than the hospital currently provides. Many of their children, who are now nearly adults, are moving to warmer climates; the majority of those remaining are employed in service sector positions. This new working population is not primarily employed by manufacturing concerns but rather by computer service companies and other businesses that use alternative means of insurance coverage past the traditional "hospitalization" used by their parents' employers. Callan's challenge is to establish business relationships with these individuals and to ensure that all of the medical needs of his patient community are met satisfactorily.

Still another lingering issue for Callan's immediate attention is a rightsizing effort proposed by Lauretta Barnes and the executive staff. While Callan agrees that a need exists to reduce staff, Barnes' proposal suggested a layoff based on tenure. That is, individuals with the greatest length of employment in the organization would keep their jobs—regardless of their performance or contribution—while new employees or those with less than two years of service would be dismissed. Callan is fundamentally against this proposal, as he believes that there are many individuals currently working in the organization who, despite their long tenure, are performing at a substandard level, while many newly hired staff members are contributing greatly. He must therefore convince the board of the folly of Barnes' layoff proposal while suggesting a more prudent course of action.

The current composition of the Forest View Hospital's board of directors presents yet another challenge for Callan. Established as a volunteer board when the hospital was founded, it currently comprises 27 members for an organization that employs 1,000 staff members. In Callan's estimation, this is unwieldy. Several of the current members are not totally committed to their responsibilities, as indicated by their lack of attendance or negligible participation at board meetings. Additionally, many board members have not kept up-to-date on current healthcare trends and issues: Several members have a difficult time understanding why the hospital does not conduct its business in the manner it did when "Larry Farmer opened the place thirty years ago."

Callan faces another dilemma, which relates specifically to the five-year-old social work department that employs 43 individuals. In examining specific case loads, Callan was distressed to find that none of the case social workers was working at a capacity of greater than 30 percent. The program was initiated to address the need for additional mental health services throughout the Forest View community, particularly in the area of geriatric care. However, it has become a monolithic entity, and its obvious overstaffing and apparent underutilization concerns not only Callan but the majority of his executive staff.

As indicated in Figure 8.1, Callan currently leads a full complement of executives. His chief financial officer, Ashlyn Tantara, has been in her position for four years after a total of ten years of service in other capacities. Tantara has worked her way steadfastly up the ranks and, in Callan's estimation, is a definite "superstar," both in terms of her leadership skills as well as her financial acumen. His chief operating officer, Nick Bonelli, is new to the organization, as he was Callan's chief operating officer at their previous employer, Chatam Memorial Hospital. The vice president of human resources, Bernie Evander, has been at the hospital for 23 years and was promoted to his position during the first year of Lauretta Barnes' tenure. He is in favor of the "tenure layoff" strategy and in fact helped Barnes to develop that plan—which is not favored by either Bonelli or Tantara.

Theresa Newport is the vice president of patient care services and has worked at Forest View Hospital for over fifteen years; she started as a nurse and progressed through the ranks to her present position. Newport is a strong advocate of outpatient services and firmly believes that the hospital must increase its ability to offer them. In fact, Newport has begun preliminary discussions with two independent outpatient clinics in the Forest View service area, both of which are led by physicians who at one time were affiliated with Forest View Hospital.

Lauretta Barnes established three additional vice president positions. Paul Callan consequently has three more executives directly reporting

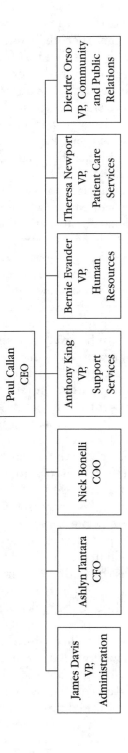

Figure 8.1 Forest View Hospital Organizational Chart

to him. Dierdre Orso is the vice president of community and public relations and has been at the hospital for seven years. Her duties include all public relations programs, communications, and assorted community activities. James Davis is the vice president of administration and has been employed by the hospital for 28 years. He oversees the cafeteria and the security force. Anthony King is the vice president for support services, and his responsibilities include management information services, the business office, and admissions. Recently, Callan asked all of the vice presidents to conduct a job component review of their specific positions and to place additional emphasis on their future accountabilities.

There are several factors that will help Callan refocus the Forest View Hospital. First, the closest competitor is 40 miles away, a considerable distance given the suburban setting of Forest View and its surrounding communities. Second, his physician group is relatively loyal, although a certain amount of fear exists because of the emergence of local HMOs. The time-honored allegiance to the community also bodes well for the hospital as it prepares for a new phase of its history.

Two other collateral issues are also favorable for Callan as he begins his transitional efforts. First, the Fairview Institute, a local mental healthcare facility, which for years was state-operated, is currently being "shopped around" by the newly elected state government. Callan feels that this might be an excellent opportunity for Forest View Hospital, as the mental health facility employs psychiatrists, clinical psychologists, and other individuals who can provide specific services. However, the state-run facility has become a "political football"—a highly visible institution spotlighted by the media—which is the reason it is currently being marketed for potential buyers.

Second, Callan believes that the majority of his employees are loyal to Forest View Hospital, recognize that the healthcare environment is changing, and are relatively receptive to adapting to a new direction that would help in providing the best healthcare possible. With the exception of two small union shops with a total membership of 175 of the 1,000 employees, the workforce is motivated, reasonably satisfied, and dedicated to the organization and its fundamental mission. It is now incumbent upon Callan and his executive team, however, to redefine that mission and make it more relevant as the hospital moves into a new era of change and increasing demands.

Transition and Transformation

After three months, Callan gained a fundamental understanding of the Forest View Hospital past the cursory information given to him in the selection and hiring process. He then began to develop a transition and transformation plan. The transition elements of his strategy would include any activities and programs that directly affected the leadership of the organization, while transformation segments would include all activities and programs that would affect the rest of the staff and set the stage for renewal. By using these two terms throughout the first year of his leadership, Callan can provide a clear set of reference points.

The first transitional strategy used by Callan is the board summit. His objective is to provide the board members, as well as the executive leadership, with a clear understanding of the hospital's direction and future orientation. Accordingly, Callan calls the board summit "Forest View 2000," a title designed to connote four basic ideas:

1. that the hospital leadership was not only focusing on the next year, but several years of progress and growth;
2. that the hospital was entering a "future-focus" stage of its development, and *all* stakeholders must focus on the future, rather than the past;
3. that the name "Forest View 2000" described an initiative for the complete transformation of the organization; and
4. knowing that the board was concerned about the hospital's three-year financial decline, Callan clearly wanted to focus on long-range planning, which would facilitate open discussion of acquisitions, collaborative arrangements, and other initiatives that would be vital to Forest View Hospital's future progress and growth.

Attendance at the board summit is mandatory for all members of the executive staff and the board of directors. This summit is conducted at a local conference facility over three days in a comfortable but not extravagant setting.

Callan opens the discussion by presenting ten specific questions, five of which are indicated in Figure 8.2. On the first day, various board sub-committees and the executive staff answer the questions raised by these ten points. On the second day, Callan deliberately mixes the groups so

Figure 8.2 Board Analytical Review Chart

Business Dimensions
What is our demographic composition?
What is your assessment of our business environment?
Do we have a positive perception among the community?
What is our future growth potential?
How can we take a proactive position?

board members and staff worked in groups discussing the same points and answering the same pertinent questions. On the third day, Callan leads a plenary group session in which all attendees discuss their outcomes, suggestions, and results. As a result, these initiatives are established:

1. The hospital would explore opportunities with the state in purchasing the mental health facility currently for sale.

2. The Forest View Hospital would undergo a necessary rightsizing effort, but it would be based on a series of criteria that would not include years of service as a primary consideration.

3. The hospital would consider collaborative arrangements with the two outpatient clinics and that this effort would be spearheaded by Theresa Newport.

4. The board of directors would examine its size, efficiency, and effectiveness within the next six months. In fact, the board committed to reorganizing itself using the schematic presented in Figure 8.3.

5. The hospital would consider a reorganization at an appropriate time within the next year, pending the outcomes of the discussions with the state regarding the mental health facility and Newport's negotiations with the outpatient clinics.

6. A major effort would be launched within the next six months to enlist the participation and input of all staff members, using some sort of survey.

7. The board would meet monthly, rather than quarterly, with executive staff to discuss key initiatives and issues, and to grant their approval for initiatives that:
   • benefited the patient;
   • benefited the organization; and
   • provided a "future focus" relative to the provision of medical and healthcare services.

8. All managers would meet at a management summit to discuss the same points listed in Figure 8.2;

9. A team of selected physicians would form a steering committee to oversee negotiations with local HMOs and insurance providers; and

10. By the end of the year, the organization would undertake a rightsizing effort, complete a restructuring, and develop a strategy for organizational renewal.

Upon returning to the hospital after the summit, Callan shifts his attention from the board to his organization. Two primary objectives become the vanguard of his next executive actions. First, he steadfastly believes that the organization should garner some current information

Figure 8.3 Forest View Hospital Board Committee Composition

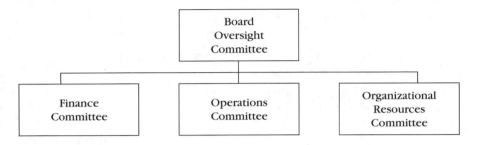

relative to the perceptions, perspectives, and opinions of the "typical Forest View healthcare consumer." To accomplish this, he assigns Dierdre Orso to conduct focus groups throughout the community. Using these groups, Callan wants to determine what the typical consumer needs, the consumer's perception of the quality of service offered by the Forest View Hospital, and the areas—both positive and negative—that concern the customer most.

In discussing this objective with Orso during a weekly executive staff meeting, Callan learns that Ashlyn Tantara, the CFO, has been collecting useful customer/patient input informally over the past year. Tantara's strategy was simple: She assigned her four directors each month to randomly call ten patients who have been discharged from the Forest View Hospital or have received outpatient services. Each director asks two basic questions:

1. What did we do "right" during your stay or while you received outpatient services?
2. What areas do we need to improve for you to feel as though we are your premier healthcare provider?

During her monthly meetings with these four directors, Tantara discusses the results of the phone calls. Usually, at least 32–35 individuals respond, and a credible assortment of information is gathered.

Callan is intrigued by this informal collection of meaningful data and suggests that this strategy might be incorporated not only by Orso in her focus groups but by all vice presidents. He assigns each vice president to call ten patients at random in the next month, and report any findings at the next monthly meeting.

The second major internal objective for Callan is to review how individual performance is assessed and how staff are compensated. From Callan's perspective, it appears that the organization uses a simple "pass/fail" performance evaluation system, which not only fails to inspire better performance but also makes the gross mistake of combining "superstar," "steady," and "nonplayer" performers into one general category. Consequently, all individuals receive an across-the-board pay increase based on a cost-of-living allowance as opposed to a bonus strategy that can give staff members the incentive to improve performance. He assigns Bernie Evander, the vice president of human resources, to review the performance evaluation system and recommend newer, better approaches within the next three months.

Callan now shifts his attention to accomplishing some of the objectives set forth in the board summit. Primarily, he is interested in engaging the employees in a discussion of their desires for the organization and their perceptions of future growth and progress. To accomplish this, he utilizes the change readiness index (CRI) instrument. Each employee is asked to complete this questionnaire, and to elicit maximum participation, Callan has decided to raffle off three prizes—a color television set, a microwave oven, and a portable compact disc player.

When an employee completes and returns the CRI survey, he or she will receive a raffle ticket as the completed survey is placed in a locked collection box. In this way, fear of retribution is assuaged, and individuals are fully encouraged to participate in this important exercise. To ensure confidentiality further, Callan hires a noted national consultant, Dr. Kyle Flanagan, to tabulate and analyze the results of this survey. Additionally, Callan contracts Flanagan to return to the facility and not only present the CRI's results but to conduct educational sessions in which they are discussed.

The CRI results are both validating and revealing for Callan and the executive staff. They indicate that most staff members—including managers, physicians, and employees alike—believe that healthcare is changing, and it is absolutely necessary for the Forest View Hospital to change as well. Additionally, the lowest negative rating on the entire survey pertains to the "nonplayers," who have been allowed to perform at substandard levels. These individuals have also been "morale busters"—the exact term used by several respondents in the survey.

The CRI results were presented to all staff members in three-hour sessions that were conducted during a two-week period two months after the survey was completed. Because the survey results were presented quickly, and education was provided by Flanagan, these sessions were well received by the managers, physicians, and other staff members. Soon after this, a two-day management summit was held in which the CRI results were reviewed and management strategies were immediately adopted. These strategies included many of the "nonplayer" management techniques, "house rules," and communication strategies that were presented in earlier chapters and in the appendix.

In addition to these techniques, each manager, supervisor, and team leader constructs timelines that listed accomplishments of their individual areas of responsibility over the past year. Callan believes that it is essential that the organization shift its focus from its various financial setbacks, which he feels have received a disproportionate amount of attention, and force the managers to refocus on the contributions, positive action, and progressive development of their individual areas of responsibility. Moreover, Callan directs Flanagan to have the managers establish timelines for the upcoming year in which new objectives and accomplishments will be defined. Timelines for one particular section are presented in Figure 8.4. At the conclusion of the management forum, Callan declares that the initial transition and transformation process has been completed. He feels that he has "transitioned" competently into his responsibilities as CEO of the Forest View Hospital and that the initial reorganization process will now lead to a reconstruction and renewal of the organization. However, he cautions that his optimism is tempered by the reality that the organization is currently overstaffed and that a rightsizing effort is necessary to stem its financial losses. He wants the managers to know that no final decisions about rightsizing have been made and that rumors, conjecture, and innuendo must be stemmed to prevent fear from spreading throughout the employee ranks.

To this end, Callan encourages all of his managers to be leaders in the true sense of the word. That is, he instructs his managers to lead aggressively and positively by:

1. presenting communication quickly, compassionately, and competently;
2. making decisions quickly, judiciously, and progressively;
3. providing education and insight to all staff members at all times; and
4. providing hands-on leadership on a daily basis by using the timelines and other initiatives during the upcoming year of transition.

Figure 8.4 Timeline for Forest View Hospital's Volunteer Corps

Volunteer Educational Summit	Staffing of New Clinics	United Way
Recruiting Drive Launch	Regional Volunteer Conference	Marine Corps Toys for Tots Drive

Callan concludes the summit by reaffirming his belief that each manager can successfully lead the organization to a bright, progressive future. He also pledges his commitment to each manager by restating his open-door policy and his belief that "Any time is a good time for an idea that will make Forest View Hospital a premier healthcare provider."

Rightsizing the Right Way

At the conclusion of Callan's first six months at the Forest View Hospital, several positive initiatives begin to affect his future plans for the organization. First, Ashlyn Tantara is very successful in achieving some cost savings through the accounting programs of the hospital, particularly in the manner in which receivables are collected and bills are reconciled. Second, Theresa Newport makes great strides in bringing the two leaders of the local outpatient clinics to the negotiating table and entering meaningful discussions about joining the Forest View Hospital. Finally, Paul Callan and Nick Bonelli, together with Leslie Summers, an influential board member, make great advances in bargaining with the state to acquire the local mental health facility.

However, the problem of overstaffing—and the unfortunate possibility of downsizing—still exists. In order to address this concern, Callan introduces six organizational initiatives:

Early retirement

Approximately sixty individuals employed by the Forest View Hospital are approaching retirement age. These individuals will not only receive the thirty-year retirement benefits afforded by the hospital but will receive a series of government benefits. Approximately fifty of these individuals are two years away from this retirement age.

Callan and the executive staff determine that these fifty individuals can enjoy their retirement benefits presently through a "bridge program" in which the organization would make up the difference between their retirement package and their current compensation. The difference between their full pension and their current full salary is favorable to the hospital and represents an appreciable cost savings. Callan makes all of these potential early retirees aware of this opportunity through a personal letter sent to each individual's home. He then encourages each one to contact Riddick Hayes, the employee relations specialist in the human resources department, to discuss the option further. He also suggests that Hayes informally contact these individuals to answer any questions they might have and to discuss the rudiments of the early retirement program further.

Thirty-eight individuals opt for early retirement, and Callan and the executive staff hold a special retirement dinner for these individuals to honor them for their accomplishments and contributions to the Forest View Hospital. Twenty of these individuals immediately join the volunteer corps to ensure their continued commitment to the hospital. In the next two years, 11 of the 12 potential early retirees take advantage of the early retirement offer, and thus save the organization a certain amount of money while retiring gracefully and respectfully.

The documentation program

While Callan has become dismayed at the considerable amount of time it is taking Bernie Evander and the human resources staff to implement a new performance evaluation system, he is even more dismayed at the lack of terminations, probations, and other disciplinary procedures used by the management staff. Accordingly, he engages Dr. Flanagan to conduct a comprehensive one-day management education session on how to document poor performance, not only in terms of quantitative job scope but also in using specific job-based performance criteria. These criteria, which include job dynamics present in virtually every position at Forest View Hospital, are clearly defined, approved by all accreditation bodies, and supported by specific defining elements. It is the responsibility of each manager, from the point of seminar presentation to when they leave the organization, to document poor performance fully, counsel "nonplayers" appropriately, and use probation and other disciplinary tactics to remove them from the Forest View Hospital.

Within six months of this seminar, Jessica Dominique, the director of radiology, receives the written resignations of two "nonplayer" employees. Callan highlights these two resignations in his monthly staff meetings, and encourages his vice presidents to ascertain how strongly the documentation program is being used in their divisions.

In another instance, Meagan Dreves, the pharmacy manager, places two employees on disciplinary probation. One of these employees, Peri Garr, files a complaint with the human resources office and her respective union leader. Upon learning this from Nick Bonelli, Dreves' immediate manager, Callan personally assures Dreves that he will fully support her disciplinary action because she clearly did the right thing.

By the end of the year, thirteen individuals have been terminated or have resigned in the face of disciplinary action from Forest View Hospital. In nine of these cases, the positions in which these individuals worked were eliminated, as a job analysis review, job component review, and management assessment indicated that the positions were not being fully utilized. As a result, the hospital recognizes a cost savings of $375,000, without any loss of service.

The hiring freeze

Another step Callan immediately takes in an effort to "rightsize the right way" is to implement a hiring freeze throughout the entire organization. In essence, any open position vacated for any reason is not filled immediately. In fact, the only way for an open position to be filled is through a formal process requiring approval up to that of the CEO himself.

The hiring freeze fulfills several objectives. First, it sends a clear, unmistakable message to all staff members that the organization is serious about saving money. Second, the freeze reassures existing employees that their jobs would not be jeopardized while new, unproven individuals were being hired. Third, the hiring freeze forces managers to review open positions and to determine exactly what staffing needs they required. Finally, the freeze indicates to the community that the hospital is reviewing its resources to better serve the patient/customers.

This last point is restated by Callan in his presentations to local community groups. Callan, in fact, makes a specific effort to increase his schedule of community interaction, so that he could establish contacts, "tell the story of the hospital," and gather as much firsthand information as possible to shape the new Forest View Hospital productively.

Social work department streamlining

After conducting an exhaustive position analysis questionnaire process throughout the social work department, and consulting extensively with Tracy MacKenzie, the department's director, Callan is convinced of that division's staff underutilization. It was apparent that during the hospital's profitable years—marked by unquestioned reimbursement and no competition—the social work department was allowed to prosper and grow beyond the point of reasonable utilization. In recent years, however, the decreased utilization, in conjunction with competition from the state's mental health facility, created the need for streamlining.

Forest View Hospital also has several psychiatrists on staff, and in informal conversations with the medical staff president, Dr. Rick Jackson, Callan learns that the demand for psychiatric care has increased throughout the Forest View community. Additionally, the small clinical psychology component of the hospital is not only fully utilized but overburdened with cases. With the possibility of a joint venture with the state mental health facility, the Fairview Institute, the likelihood of an increased demand for the services provided by social workers appears remote.

In discussing the situation with Tracy MacKenzie, it becomes evident to Callan that she is somewhat close-minded in terms of streamlining and is unyielding in her demands to increase the department into specialty areas that appear to have no specific market-driven mandate. Because MacKenzie does not suggest any progressive solutions to this vexing problem, Callan provides her with four options:

1. effect a 40 percent reduction in force in the social work department, based strictly on tenure;
2. effect a 40 percent reduction in force within the department, based on merit, using the institution's somewhat arcane performance evaluation instrument;
3. effect a reduction of 40 percent using a new performance evaluation system, which has been developed by Riddick Hayes, the employee relations specialist; or
4. provide a comprehensive strategic plan in which the social work department can be streamlined into the Fairview Institute.

Unfortunately, after a week of deliberation, MacKenzie decides that she would rather resign than accept any of these options. Callan accepts MacKenzie's resignation and appoints Denise Branch—the assistant director of the social work department—as acting director. After reviewing the four options with Branch, Callan encourages her to come up with her own solution, given the need to reduce the staff by 40 percent. Branch suggests that many of the social workers would voluntarily accept part-time status at the institution, as many are interested in spending more time with their families or establishing their own practice. In either case, the security of the benefits package afforded by part-time status can create a "safety net" for these two categories of social workers. Additionally, Branch decides to use the six-month performance evaluation system, as the new form mandates that each social worker describe his or her job components, set an action plan for the coming year, and basically maintain accountability for individual practices within the department (Lombardi 1993).

For the present time, Callan and Branch decide that this strategy is the best incremental approach to streamlining the social work department.

Position and job content review and analysis

Using the social work department's experiment as a catalyst, Callan decides that every individual within the organization will complete a comprehensive position analysis, similar to the exercise suggested in the early chapters of this book. The objective of this process is twofold: First, Callan can determine if in fact all of the organizational members of Forest View Hospital are being completely utilized. Second, the job content review provides the individual and collective foundation for the new criterion-based performance evaluation system that is being developed by Riddick Hayes.

After completing this six-month process, and reviewing all of the positions in conjunction with his executive staff, Callan decides that there are at least forty full-time positions that can be converted to part-time ones. Accordingly, the organization first asks all employees to shift voluntarily from full- to part-time status, recognizing that benefits will be maintained for the part-time individuals while a cost savings will be realized in salaries. After receiving a dozen volunteers, Callan then makes the tough call and converts thirty job positions from full-time to part-time. This achieves the necessary fiscal savings.

An additional result of the conversion from full-time to part-time based on the position analysis review is another group of employees who seek early retirement. Among these is Bernie Evander, the vice president of human resources, who, although not affected by the conversion, has nonetheless decided to opt for the early retirement package, which he says "looks better and better as he reviews it with employees." With the good fortune of having Riddick Hayes, the employee relations specialist, as a logical, positive, and contributing replacement for Evander, Callan gladly accepts Evander's resignation and promotes Hayes into the director of human resources position. Therefore, the first major change at the executive level during Callan's tenure, despite all of the financial problems and current rightsizing initiatives, results in an internal organizational member being promoted to the top of his respective career ladder while his predecessor is allowed to exit the organization gracefully and reap a well-deserved pension.

The six-month review program

Callan redefines the organization's compensation program upon installation of Riddick Hayes' new criterion-based performance evaluation system. As the new system assesses not only *what* the employees do, but *how* they do it—that is, the evaluation considers their adaptability, compassion, and technical expertise, for example, as well as their actual job performance—the system takes shape as a more effective "paid for performance system." Accordingly, Callan decides that three basic levels of performance will be established and serve as the reference point for compensation:

1. **Above expectations**, as clearly demonstrated on the performance evaluation, which will result in four extra vacation days during the review year;
2. **Meets expectations**, as clearly established on the performance evaluation, which will result in not only the cost-of-living adjustment but two additional vacation days; and
3. **Below expectations**, which will result in an automatic three-month disciplinary probation.

Callan decides that the first cycle of performance evaluation will not be a full year, but six months into the process. As state and jurisdictional accreditation bodies support this, he enacts a program in which all staff will be reviewed after a six-month period. Subsequent to this review, all employees will be reviewed on the anniversary date of the day they entered their current job position. In this manner, all performance evaluations become exclusive and specifically relevant to the individual's work history at Forest View Hospital.

After the initial six-month review, Callan discovers that 37 employees have been rated as performing below expectations. These individuals immediately go on automatic disciplinary probation, and after three months, all have either resigned or been terminated for cause. More importantly, however, the employees who received the two or four extra days off—depending on their relative performance—clearly appreciate the new system, which is merit-based and thus provides greater incentive for better work.

In undertaking these six programs, Callan not only reduces his workforce considerably but reaps the intended financial benefits of a streamlined organization. As a result, Forest View Hospital is well positioned not only to survive in the future but thrive and experience the positive benefits of expansion and growth.

The Reconstruction Process

With the rightsizing process completed, Callan and the executive staff turn their attention to restructuring the organization. From the beginning they face two interesting situations. First, Theresa Newport has been able to broker an agreement for a collaborative arrangement with the two outpatient clinics in the Forest View community area. The first, the Lennox Park Clinic, is run by a physician, Dr. Sonny West, who is amenable to a protracted, incremental "buyout" of the facility in exchange for employment of his staff and an incentive-laden contract. This meets with the approval of Forest View Hospital, particularly after it is ratified by the organization's legal counsel, Jeffrey Marmora. The second clinic, at Lewis Beach—a small community fifteen miles from Forest View—is run by Craig Stevens, a physical therapist manager, and staffed by forty employees. The Lewis Beach clinic offers several possibilities to the Forest View organization, as it can act as a springboard for expansion of services past its nominal physical therapy services.

Additionally, Craig Stevens has established a strong home care program under the auspices of the Lewis Beach clinic. Because Stevens has run the home care component for several years, and is extremely knowledgeable about home health care, Callan and his executives see an extra benefit in his recruitment to the Forest View organization.

Second, Callan and the board have completed their agreement with the state regarding the Fairview Institute. The state government, in its haste to divest itself of the clinic—and with recent political change at the top levels of state government—has agreed to a deal that is most favorable to Forest View. As a result, Callan rechristens the facility the Forest View Institute to clearly denote that it is no longer a state-run organization, and it will enjoy the legacy, traditions, and high quality of service of Forest View Hospital.

Along with the absorption of the Institute came the problem of how to absorb the former employees. As a starting point, Callan institutes the performance evaluation system at the Institute and makes all of the employees aware of the needs and expectations of the Forest View organization. By using town hall meetings, newsletters, and other such communication methods, Callan ensures that all Forest View Institute staff understand that a new direction will be established for their facility. As part of his agreement with the state, Callan provides outplacement services to individuals who decide not to remain with the new Forest View Institute. Additionally, the state has allowed these individuals to transfer to other state-run facilities if desired. Most of the employees, however, decide to stay and "give Forest View a shot," in the words of one employee.

Because the Forest View Institute provides mental health services, Callan considers the possibility, after discussions with Denise Branch, to move the social work component to the new facility. This move is endorsed by Dr. Rick Jackson, who believes that the facilities, remote campus location, and other specific features of the Institute would afford greater service. Putting the needs of the patient first, the social work department, clinical psychology staff, and practicing psychiatrists affiliated with Forest View Hospital all move to the Forest View Institute.

Following the successful rightsizing and using the new energy infused by the new staff of the Forest View Institute, Callan decides to reorganize the entire facility. He has five objectives during the reorganization:

1. to use the good name of Forest View Hospital as much as possible;
2. to use the new talent brought about by the acquisitions and the recent internal changes within the hospital;
3. to establish a new organizational structure that focuses on the patient's needs;
4. to establish an organizational structure that will maintain clarity and simplicity through the change process; and
5. to create an organizational structure that will serve the Forest View Hospital usefully, practically, and realistically in the coming years—not only its daily operations, but also in the interests of encouraging the "Forest View 2000" initiative.

As indicated on Figure 8.5, Callan implements a patient-focus model, which is a hybrid of several of the models delineated in Chapter 5 of this book. As illustrated in the figure, several organizational objectives are achieved. First, the simplicity of the model is founded on its intent to make things simple for the patient.

Second, the names and titles used in the model are nonthreatening. For example, in no regard is the word "support" used. Rather, all of the patient-focus lines are denoted as "systems." Callan, the board of directors, and in fact the entire leadership desired to delineate systems that are interdependent, cohesive, and contributory to a larger system

Figure 8.5   Forest View Hospital's Patient-Focus Model

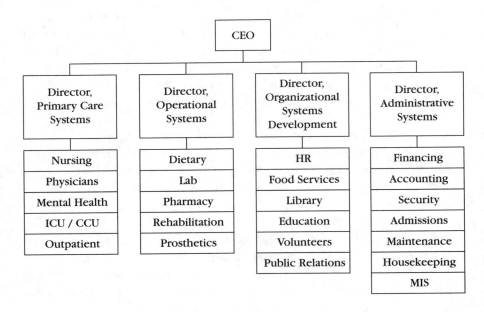

capable of meeting the demands of the community's customer/patients in an exemplary manner.

Furthermore, the model allows Callan the opportunity to provide greater responsibility for his emerging executive talent. Craig Stevens, Dr. Rick Jackson, Nick Bonelli, and Denise Branch will all have new reporting responsibilities and increased, challenging accountabilities. Most notably, Riddick Hayes has moved into a position that will allow him the greatest amount of professional growth and development conceivable in a healthcare organization.

With the board's approval, Callan has decided to call the new organization "The Forest View Healthcare System." This new title incorporates the Forest View name, includes the "system approach" for the new organization, and gives Callan the flexibility to let the Institute, Lewis Beach, and the Lennox Park facilities take advantage of the Forest View name.

To make certain that all staff members of the renewed Forest View Healthcare System understand the model, Callan uses several approaches to ensure that he communicates efficiently. First, a guidebook is published by the public relations department for distribution to all staff as well as community members. This guidebook features the history of the Forest View Healthcare System and details the new organization. With the statement, "Our celebrated past emboldens our way to the future," a new motto is enacted in conjunction with the launch of the new organizational model. Furthermore, Callan prepares a script, with the assistance of Dr. Kyle Flanagan, that will help the managers in their monthly staff meetings answer specific questions regarding the new system, its effect on their individual job responsibilities, and other pressing questions.

Additionally, Callan posts an organizational chart depicting the new system at entry points in all of the facilities, including employee entrances, patient entrances, patient waiting areas, and other such points. On these charts, particular services are listed, without titles or other intricacies. Finally, Callan ensures that a new phone book, organizational directory, and other "basics" are developed.

Because of the strategic plan created by Callan and the Forest View leadership during the transition and transformation stage, Callan's work in the reconstruction effort has been relatively simple and straightforward. The reorganization worked seamlessly because of the work done prior to the creation of the model.

The Renewal Process

To complete the reorganization process successfully, the executive staff at Forest View Healthcare Systems institute 23 programs relative to the renewal effort. In this last section, we will discuss each, which were generated by input from staff and community members.

1. **The change assessment index.** At the end of the first year of his tenure, Callan conducts a change assessment index. Using many of the same factors as the change readiness index, this instrument allows a comprehensive review of how the organization is doing. Additionally, it acts as a wellspring of new ideas, suggestions, and solutions the new Forest View organization could use.

2. **Volunteer greeters.** One of the suggestions from the change assessment index is to use greeters at each entry point of all of the facilities. These volunteer greeters would help visitors and patients find the specific department they needed. Based on a similar program used by a local retail store, these greeters would act as ambassadors to the customer/patient community.

3. **Gold-grams.** Many staff members indicated that they did not always know about organizational issues. As a result, Callan decides to issue gold-grams—gold being the predominant color in Forest View signage—as a way to convey essential information to all members of the organization. Additionally, he tells all employees to believe that whenever a gold-gram was issued, "The information was as good as gold." That is, the employees could rely on the gold-grams more than gossip, rumors, or other communication spread by "nonplayers."

4. **Show-and-tell sessions.** With the incorporation of new facilities into the Forest View Healthcare System, Callan thinks it is essential that all components know their new colleagues and counterpart groups. Therefore, he establishes "show-and-tell sessions" in which all facilities and departments present their basic structure, service orientation, and range of technical expertise to their new colleagues. For example, Craig Stevens arranged the first session, in which staff from the Lewis Beach clinic—now the Forest View Clinic at Lewis Beach—gave a brief overview of their operation to the main hospital.

5. **The new credo.** In addition to the motto for the new system, Callan, with input provided by the change assessment index, implements a new credo for the Forest View Health System. This new credo has five basic points:

- The customer/patient is our primary motivation and inspiration.
- We find our strength in each other in our daily mission.
- Excellence of execution is an everyday objective.
- Patient care and quality is everyone's responsibility.
- Nobody succeeds unless we all succeed.

This credo is printed on attractive parchment paper, framed, and displayed prominently, in conjunction with the organization's new motto, throughout all Forest View facilities.

6. **The Board/Management summit.** At the outset of the second year of his tenure, Callan brings both the board and management team of the Forest View Healthcare System together for a major summit, where the ten points posed to both groups at the previous year's summits, are discussed jointly. In doing this, Callan establishes commonalities regarding the viewpoints and perspectives of board members and managers. Furthermore, he is able to delineate his common vision for the system and review the timelines that were presented by his managers. Moreover, Callan provides a timeline plan for the future actions of the organization and uses this as the genesis of the organization's new strategic plan.

7. **Fact sheets.** With the emergence of the new organization, Callan instructs Dierdre Orso to construct a fact sheet on the new system, which includes information on all of the components of Forest View Healthcare System and provides essential contact information for patients and employees alike.

8. **Departmental fact sheets.** In addition to the organizational fact sheets, Callan instructs each manager to create a fact sheet for his or her individual department and service. These fact sheets would then be distributed throughout the organization and would contain four basic components:

- The department's mission;
- The department's location;
- The services provided by the department; and
- The individuals who provide those services.

The fact sheets are beneficial not only to patients seeking information but staff members who desire information on the new organizational structure and, more particularly, how that structure affects its individual departments and jobs.

9. **The geriatric program.** With a widespread elderly population throughout Forest View service communities, the need for geriatric services was becoming more and more apparent. As a result, Callan designates a task force consisting of employees, managers, board members, and community members to recommend various geriatric awareness programs. Forest View Healthcare System, as a result of the task force's findings, enters into an agreement with a local intergenerational day care center. Furthermore, several preventive programs relating to cancer, heart disease, and other afflictions are also recommended.

10. **The Forest View intergenerational day care center.** After a disappointing experience with the local intergenerational day care provider, Callan decides to renovate space once used as inpatient rooms into an in-house intergenerational day care center. By using his existing resources from his children's day care center, and by obtaining a grant from the state using the contacts he made during the Fairview Institute acquisition, Callan establishes an intergenerational day care center, which is fully used by both employees and community members alike. This center provides employment opportunities for senior citizens who can obtain the necessary credentials as day care providers.

11. **Fan mail bulletin boards.** Fan mail bulletin boards are quickly established at every Forest View facility. Furthermore, a central fan mail bulletin board, which contains correspondence directed to Callan himself or to board members, is erected at the hospital's cafeteria. However, if any correspondence relates to a specific facility of the organization, it is not only sent to that institution but also highlighted in the organization's newsletter. Shortly after the implementation of the fan mail bulletin boards, similar bulletin boards begin to "spring up" in individual departments, wards, and offices throughout the facility.

12. **The timeline book.** After the first quarter of the second year of Callan's tenure as CEO, all managers throughout the Forest View system construct timelines to include in a timeline book, which become the organization's annual report. A copy is then distributed to each staff member. In doing so, staff gauge the progress of not only their departments or sections, but of the entire organization.

13. **Team of the month.** Each month, Callan sends an executive memo—not a gold-gram—to all staff celebrating the team of the month. Over the course of the first four months of his second year, such teams include the restructured social work department, the pharmacy department, the physical therapists at the Forest View–Lewis Beach facility, and the security force at Forest View Hospital. These teams are congratulated for their contribution and their importance to the overall organization is reviewed. Furthermore, the team of the month is featured in the organization's new newsletter.

14. *The Forest View Falcon.* A new newsletter is needed, in the estimation of Stevens, Sonny West, Callan, and other members of the executive cadre. The reasoning is that the hospital newsletter seemed somewhat exclusionary, not by design but by necessity, and that several of the other components of the organization have, heretofore, produced their own newsletter. As a result, Callan decides that it would be a good allocation of financial resources to innovate a new newsletter. Because the

falcon is a bird indigenous to the area, and the mascot of a now-defunct but deeply beloved local minor league baseball team, the name for the newsletter is a natural. In fact, the leadership comically takes advantage of the defunct baseball team saying, "The falcon flies again," as the launch slogan for the new newsletter.

15. **The patient assessment index.** The patient assessment index is used by the Forest View Healthcare System during Callan's second year. Similar to the patient readiness index, 500 patients are randomly asked to rate the organization. The results are published in *The Falcon* and spread through Callan's town hall meetings. The results of the index, while not entirely favorable, are generally positive and a good source of renewed morale and motivation for the institution. In areas that warrant special concern—as noted by the respondents—Callan installs quick-fix measures such as new signs, additional patient guides, and informational brochures.

16. **Founder's Day.** Forest View Hospital was founded in 1956 by Matthew Belmar, a local trucking magnate. Mr. Belmar, though retired and living in Florida, is still an honorary member of the board and often regales Callan with the story of how the hospital began in an abandoned school building; he often marvels at the hospital's success over the next forty years. Because the hospital was incorporated in October, Callan decides that a Founder's Day celebration—held annually—would be appropriate. Because the weather would still be amenable, Founder's Day would include a barbecue where the managers prepared and served food to the employees, both during the day shift as well as the off shifts. Additionally, the annual report, containing all of the timelines, would be distributed. This is also a logical time as the hospital operated on a fiscal year of October to September.

17. **Streamlining the board.** Asking the board of directors to consider the twenty points of the strategic action plan was the beginning of its streamlining. Many board members decide that their interest in the hospital had waned, and they gracefully accept early retirement. Additionally, Callan is able to effect his new board structure, as delineated in Figure 8.3. In fact, two board members of the two clinics are made members of the new Forest View Healthcare System board. By creating both a system board as well as a hospital board, Callan preserves the dignity of hospital board members who do not wish to retire while reaping the benefits of the flexibility of a newer, more progressive system board.

18. **Physician acquisitions.** With the assistance of Dr. Sonny West and Dr. Rick Jackson, Callan purchases several local physician practices. Specific requirements have to be met for a practice to be acquired,

including the scope of the practice, its applicability to at least two of the Forest View facilities, the potential of the individual physician as a leader and manager, and naturally, the current marketing and financial strength of the individual practice. These guidelines ensure the fiscal benefit to all of the physician acquisitions.

19. **Suggestion standards.** Callan changes the suggestion box system to include five basic parameters. All suggestions—which would be eligible for a $100, $200, or $300 bonus, depending on their applicability and usefulness—must meet five basic standards:

- practicality;
- reasonability;
- viability;
- specificity; and
- progressivity.

Any suggestions that meet all five of these guidelines are eligible for financial renumeration and highlighting in *The Forest View Falcon*.

20. **Organizational bonuses.** At the conclusion of the second year of Callan's tenure, the institution actually finds itself in the enviable position of being "in the black." Accordingly, Callan is able to award bonuses, based on yearly performance, in the form of a savings bond. Individuals whose performance "met expectations" receive a $250 bond, while staff members who performed at an "above expectations" level receive a $500 bond. Those individuals who were "below expectations" still receive a three-month disciplinary probation.

21. **Monthly staff meeting.** Monthly staff meetings become a requisite of management and staff performance throughout the organization, and are replete with discussions of the rumor of the month, the win of the month, the learning point of the month, and the major organizational issue of the month.

22. **Closed circuit television.** The existing closed circuit television capacity in both the Forest View Institute and the main hospital is used not only to promote patient education but provide various in-service educational programs to employees. This video capacity also allows videotapes to be checked out of the learning resources center for use at home by staff.

23. **Medical center designation.** After going through the proper legal and jurisdictional channels, Callan upgrades the hospital's status to that of medical center. Accordingly, the "Forest View Medical Center" is now the cornerstone of the entire Forest View Healthcare System.

Callan's 23 initiatives not only redirect the organization but in conjunction with the rightsizing and reconstruction effort, create a renewed, successful healthcare system.

Reference

Lombardi, D. N. 1993. *Handbook for the New Health Care Manager*. Chicago: American Hospital Publishing.

MANAGING NONPLAYER RESISTANCE TO CHANGE

T he greatest threat to organizational renewal is the nonplayer's attempt to undermine the change effort. As we have discussed, a nonplayer is an individual whose performance might be barely adequate but whose behavior in the healthcare institution can be described as subversive, apathetic, or self-interested. Nonplayers become particularly fearful during all stages of organizational renewal, as they will now have more responsibility and must work harder—and smarter—than before.

In a failing healthcare organization, nonplayers are condoned because leadership lacks the fortitude to confront them. In a sense, managers who accept the nonplayers' detrimental behavior are not qualified for leadership in today's healthcare environment, where the nonplayers can cause poor morale, poor service, or in extreme situations, death.

In this section, we will discuss the twenty excuses most often used by nonplayers to derail the renewal process. For each one, we will define its basic psychology, and provide a field-proven, effective strategy to counter it.

Line 1: "You don't like me!"

Basic Psychology:

A favorite nonplayer strategy is to make all work issues personal. When nonplayers are asked to work harder for the renewed organization, they will try to make it a personal issue between the manager and themselves, not a business imperative. Because most managers want to be liked, they fall prey to this particular tactic. It is more important to be understood and respected, however, than liked and accepted.

Recommended Response: "It is not an issue of whether I like you personally or not; what I don't like is your performance, and here's two examples to discuss." At this point, the manager should present—honestly and accurately—two examples of how the nonplayer is ineffective, incompetent, or inadequate.

Line 2: "If my performance is so bad, maybe I should quit."

Basic Psychology:

The nonplayer recognizes that most managers want to help and assist their employees. Nonplayers therefore believe that, in the opinion of a manager, the greatest failure can be the resignation of an employee.

Recommended Response: "If you've decided that you cannot meet the performance expectations that we now hold for all individuals in your position, I will accept your resignation immediately." This reply shifts the accountability for the nonplayer's future actions from the manager to the nonplayer. By using the pronoun "we," the personal issue is removed and replaced by the business issue of whether the nonplayer wants to meet the new organization's requirements. In most cases, the nonplayer will not resign, but in some happy instances they may. Under no circumstances should a resigning nonplayer be rehired. In the majority of cases, this will be the last time that the nonplayer plays this particular game.

Line 3: "I've got a problem with that."

Basic Psychology:

As we have discussed, this is a favorite trick of the nonplayer. The nonplayer's intent is to force the manager to wrestle with a problem that cannot be solved—thus losing credibility with the nonplayer, as well as the rest of the staff.

Recommended Response: "A solution to our problem would be more useful, and a better use of our time. Can you provide one?" Again, this places accountability for problem solving where it should be—with the individual employee. If the employee can recognize a problem, certainly he or she is intelligent enough to suggest a solution.

Line 4: "We tried that before but it didn't work."

Basic Psychology:

Here the nonplayer is focusing on the old organizational structure and attempting to dredge up unfortunate past history.

Recommended Response: "Tell me what will work *now*." This forces the nonplayer to deal with the "here and now" of the renewed organization; it also sets a precedent that the past is only useful if it is positive.

Line 5: "If it ain't broke, don't fix it."

Basic Psychology:

A nonplayer is threatened with anything that is new and more demanding, as well as unfamiliar. Accordingly, they resist *any* form of change.

Recommended Response: "_____ just had to down-size because of that type of thinking." The manager should cite any well-known healthcare organization that was forced to dismiss any number of employees—and unfortunately there are many. This response demonstrates to nonplayers—as well as the other staff—downsizing of the wrong kind occurs when individuals wait to be "acted upon," instead of being proactive.

Line 6: "I'm different."

Basic Psychology:

Most nonplayers have usually been employed by the organization for a considerable amount of time. Therefore, they believe that they should be treated specially because of their tenure and experience. Rather than trying to force the nonplayer into uniformity with the rest of their colleagues, the manager should exploit the "differences" of the nonplayer tactfully.

Recommended Response: "And I would expect more from someone of your experience and tenure." This again places the burden for positive action and progressive thought on the nonplayer. Because most nonplayers dwell in negativity, this effectively negates his or her complaint.

Line 7: "It's not on my job description."

Basic Psychology:

Most nonplayers can cite their job description completely and use it as an excuse for not assuming new duties. The manager can ask the nonplayer to redefine their job description by using the position analysis techniques described earlier.

Recommended Response: "All of us recognize that our job descriptions only cover 70 percent of our actual responsibilities. Let's talk about the duties all of us are now expected to perform." This response sends a strong message to nonplayers that a wider range of responsibilities will be expected of them and that they are part of a cohesive, interdependent unit, not simply individuals entitled to a paycheck for only doing 70 percent (or less) of their job in the renewed organization. Remember, as no job description reflects all of a job position's scope, strict adherence to that description is, in reality, dereliction of duty.

Line 8: "That won't work."

Basic Psychology:

Most nonplayers enjoy creating doubt, suspicion, and apprehension in the workplace, which reflects their overall negativity and general dissension with positive work goals.

Recommended Response: "What *will* work?" Once again, the manager must shift the focus from redefining the problem to solving it.

Line 9: "We've always done it that way."

Basic Psychology:

The nonplayer loves to dwell in the past.

Recommended Response: "There will be more change in healthcare in the next two years than ever before—that way won't get it done anymore." This recommended response can be followed by a reminder that the organization has just gone through an extensive renewal process to come up with a new, better way of doing business. Either the nonplayer will be part of the solution, or he or she will become an ineffective part of the problem—and be treated as such.

Line 10: "Several of us think that _____."

Basic Psychology:

The nonplayer is trying to enlist group support for negativity and contentiousness.

Recommended Response: "That's probably just your opinion." And it probably is. Many managers make the mistake of asking, "Who else believes this?" which plays into the hands of the nonplayer, who then answers, "Well, that's confidential." By stripping the nonplayer of perceived group support, he or she is isolated correctly.

Line 11: "I'm stressed!"

Basic Psychology:

The nonplayer is using stress—a valid feature in the healthcare workplace, especially during reorganization—as an excuse for nonperformance.

Recommended Response: "Give me a specific example," or, "The patient is the only person owed a stressless existence." Unless the nonplayer can provide a specific example of how they are unduly affected by stress, this is again merely an excuse—not an honest work concern.

Line 12: "I'm not comfortable with that."

Basic Psychology:

The nonplayer is using the issue of job comfort—which could be legitimate—in a nonvalid manner.

Recommended Response: "What will make you more comfortable?" or, "The patient is the only individual owed comfort." Once again, the manager must seek to make the complaint specific, work related, and legitimate, or handle it as it probably is: a sneaky excuse for nonperformance.

Line 13: "That's not professional."

Basic Psychology:

Most nonplayers confuse professionalism with their intention to do things the way they want to do them.

Recommended Response: "Define professionalism for us." A nonplayer will have a difficult time doing this, and merely revert to reciting how he or she has been victimized by the new system. Once again, by using "we" or "us" instead of "me" or "I," the manager can negate this nonplayer tactic.

Line 14: "The new organization does not provide quality service."

Basic Psychology:

With the emphasis placed on quality in recent years in the healthcare environment, the nonplayer can suggest that the reason for his or her non-performance is the inability of the renewed organization to provide the customer/patient quality service: that is, they state that the institution— *not* the nonplayer—is not performing well.

Recommended Response: "If what we're planning takes better care of the customer/patient, how is it *not* quality?!" Put simply, the manager is asking the nonplayer to "either top it or drop it," rather than discussing theories of quality, which would be both a waste of time and energy.

Line 15: "Communication is a big problem!"

Basic Psychology:

As we have discussed at various times throughout this book, communication is a nebulous characteristic and thus can be cited by a nonplayer as a problem at almost every conceivable juncture.

Recommended Response: "If I tell you when to do something, how to do something, what to do, and give you communication in a style that is understandable, I have not failed you, you have failed us." The power of pronouns, action-orientation, and literally all fifteen of the leadership renewal imperatives are used in this response.

Line 16: "You won't let me talk."

Basic Psychology:

The nonplayer is suggesting that the manager is trying to prevent him or her from speaking, when really the manager is probably trying to curtail complaining.

Recommended Response: "I'll let you talk. We just don't need to hear constant complaining and whining." The best solution, obviously, is to be honest and direct in calling the nonplayer's behavior exactly what it is—unnecessary complaining.

Line 17: "You're racist/sexist/etc."

Basic Psychology:

The nonplayer is maliciously trying to interject illegalities into the work discussion.

Recommended Response: "If you truly believe that I treat you differently than other individuals in your work position, we will postpone this discussion until I can get a third party to join us." Under no condition should managers try to handle this without the assistance of at least their manager, if not the CEO. At that point, the nonplayer should prove discrimination by concrete examples, or be properly documented for slandering the manager.

Line 18: "We don't take care of the patient anymore."

Basic Psychology:

The nonplayer is trying to use patient focus to further their selfish interests.

Recommended Response: "The entire purpose of the renewed organization is to take better care of the customer/patient, as most of us understand." By citing the renewal process, and in the absence of specific examples by the nonplayer, the manager additionally enlists the unspoken support of all staff for the renewed organization.

Line 19: "All of us are scared."

Basic Psychology:

Once again, the nonplayer is trying to derail organizational renewal by suggesting that everyone is afraid of the process.

Recommended Response: "Unfortunately, I think you're wrong, because it is quite apparent to me that most of the staff committed to the renewed organization, as evidenced by their recent actions and behavior." Once again, the manager is specifying that this complaint is centered on the nonplayer, not on the work group.

Line 20: "I liked it better in the past."

Basic Psychology:

Apparently, the nonplayer, who now has more responsibilities, would love a return to the past. This is inconceivable, unrealistic, and foolhardy.

Recommended Response: "As we have discussed over the past several months, a new organization is necessary for the new demands that our patient and our community have for us." Notice that the emphasis is on *patient, community, change,* and *renewed organizational strength*—which is exactly where it should be.

While this is not an all-inclusive list, these twenty excuses are among the more obvious games that the nonplayer plays. By applying a certain degree of common sense and fortitude when using these responses, the nonplayer's affect can be diminished—if not nullified—during the entire organizational renewal process.

INDEX

ABOUT THE AUTHOR

Donald N. Lombardi, Ph.D., is the principal partner of CHR/InterVista, a healthcare management consulting firm based in Mt. Arlington, New Jersey. He attended Fordham University and received his bachelor's degree in English (1976) from Florida International University, his master's degree in human resources management (1978) from Pepperdine University, his Ph.D. in industrial psychology (1983) from the University of Missouri at St. Louis, and he completed postdoctorate work (1984) at the University of Pennsylvania.

Dr. Lombardi is a regular faculty member for the American College of Healthcare Executives and has written six of that organization's accreditation courses. He has designed and implemented management systems and reorganization programs at over 150 healthcare organizations in all fifty states and in ten foreign countries. Prior to his consulting work, Dr. Lombardi held top human resources positions at American Hospital Supply Corporation and Bristol-Myers, where he was instrumental in implementing organizational systems in American, Caribbean, and European operations.

As an officer in the United States Marine Corps, Lombardi instituted numerous educational and organizational systems, which were lauded by both military and civilian experts. He holds over fifty U.S. copyrights on organizational management systems, has written eight books, and is the author of over forty journal articles. Dr. Lombardi is also a senior fellow of the Governance Institute and is the associate director of the Masters in Health Administration Program at Seton Hall University.